The Roles of the Christian Husband

Geary Reid

Acknowledgments

Great thanks must be expressed to the following people:

The heavenly Father, for granting me the wisdom and inspiration to record the information in this book, which I began on January 17, 2022, and completed on January 19, 2022; my family, for their continued encouragement and support regarding various challenges; and several people who have assisted with reviewing and editing the book:

- Wonnetta Nicholson, Dipl. in Business Management and Administration
- Rendell F. Harry
- Joyce Sullivan

To you, the reader: have fun while reading, and grasp and practice what you learn so that this world will become a better place. Many people are depending on your guidance. We all need a shoulder to lean on and a hand to guide us.

Rev. Geary Reid

MBA, FCCA, FAAPM, MPM, CAT

Reid's Learning Institute and Business Consultancy

reidnlearn.com

Amazon: amazon.com/author/gearyreid

Facebook: Reid n Learn

Instagram: Reid n Learn

LinkedIn: Reid's Learning Institute
and Business Consultancy

199 Kuru - Kururu, Soesdyke Linden Highway
Guyana, South America

Table of Contents

Introduction

God desires for Christian husbands to be great examples to many men and women. However, many persons have misunderstood the roles of the Christian husband. Even some Christian husbands are not aware of what their roles are, and sadly, they look to their wives for guidance to identify their roles.

This literature is carefully divided into three critical sections. The first section distinguishes a man from a husband, as the role of a husband is different from the role of a man. The basic qualities of a husband are also discussed here.

Within the second section, the focus is on the husband's roles. These roles are numerous, and many persons often underestimate them. First, husbands must know that they are leaders. When a husband lives up to that role, everyone in his family will be moving in the same direction as they follow his leadership. Besides being leaders, husbands are also motivators and supporters to their wives. Many wives go through challenges, and they often look to their husbands for motivation and support. The Bible speaks about romance and sex, but many believers do not like to read what it says about these important areas of family life; this literature will show the importance of understanding and following what the Bible says about these matters. Finally, husbands are protectors and providers. The needs of the family are often met through the husband's contributions. Husbands are also expected to protect their wives, their children, and the family's possessions.

While wives are often known for communication, men must learn to be good communicators as well. Husbands may not like to talk much, but they can be good listeners and engage in non-verbal communication. When the family needs ideas, husbands ought to provide long-term plans for the family's success. Some of these long-term plans will require the husband's financial contributions, especially in homes where the husband is the primary or sole provider. Additionally, more Christian husbands must set aside time for family devotions.

When husbands are involved in domestic activities, they allow their wives to have some time to rest, and some wives will even boast that their husbands are great chefs and know how to keep the house clean. Many Christian wives appreciate the support of their husbands in assisting with domestic activities so that th\ey can spend more time doing the work of the Lord. Raising children is not a responsibility left to mothers alone, but something that fathers must also do.

The Bible reminds husbands to deal with their wives according to knowledge. Therefore, husbands must love their wives and study them. When husbands respect their wives at home and in public places, their marriages will be more comfortable. Husbands must help their wives to be healthy and stay in shape, and they must also celebrate their wives' godly qualities.

The third section challenges Christian wives to celebrate their husbands as well. It is not easy to perform many of the roles of the Christian husband, and many husbands continuously make sacrifices. Therefore, their efforts and contributions must be acknowledged and celebrated. Wives must not hold back in celebrating their husbands, as they must not allow anyone else to do what they must do.

Section 1: Distinguishing a man from a husband

There is a difference between a man and a husband, as not all men are husbands. Therefore, every husband must know who he is and be the best husband he is called to be.

Every man looking for a woman to be his wife must demonstrate certain essential qualities. Those important qualities will cause women of high quality to be attracted to them, and each man must choose one such woman to be his wife. At that point, he is expected to treat her as his companion and the person he will spend his future with.

God saw that Adam was working hard and was dedicated to his work, so God blessed him with Eve to be his wife. This was the first marriage known to man. When Eve was created, she provided support to her husband, since she was his helper, and together they had children. God only blessed Adam with one wife, because he knew that Eve was sufficient for Adam.

Married men must focus on their wives and avoid things and activities that would disturb their marriage. In addition, when men are married, they may not be able to spend as much time with their friends, parents, and siblings, as they have to invest more time in their new family.

Some men are afraid that after they get married, they will lose their identity and no longer do many of the things they once did. However, when they marry, men make commitments to be there for their families, so they will have to give up some temporary things in order to raise a successful family. The success of many families is dependent upon men understanding and performing their roles as fathers.

1. Understanding the man

To understand the husband's roles, it is essential to understand the man. In every husband, there is a man, so knowing more about the man will clarify what a husband does and who he is.

1.1 Single men

Not all men will become husbands. Some men are contented to live a single life. Other men are interested in having children to call them fathers, but they do not want to marry the mothers of their children.

If a man is coerced into marriage, then he will physically be in the marriage, but his mind will be outside of it. Therefore, every man who wants a wife must make a personal decision to choose his companion and then make that final decision of marriage.

1.2 Married men

Marriage is both a lifetime commitment and a legal one, and many men do not want that combination. Some men need companions, but they do not want to be committed to a marriage. Therefore, if they are married but do not like something about their marriage, they will pursue alternative options. It is flawed thinking for men to run away from their marriage when they do not get their way. Working men know that if they do not like what happens to them one day, they cannot stop working: they must work through each day's challenge and continue to be a great employee. Similarly, a man must not run away from his marriage when things do not work in his favor. He must be a committed person if he wants to be a good husband.

It is believed by many religious leaders that the first union of marriage took place between Adam and Eve, as recorded in Genesis 2:18-25.

While Adam was working for the Lord, God provided Adam with a helper.

Genesis 2:18-25

[18] And the LORD God said, It is not good that the man should be alone; I will make him an help meet for him. [19] And out of the ground the LORD God formed every beast of the field, and every fowl of the air; and brought them unto Adam to see what he would call them: and whatsoever Adam called every living creature, that was the name thereof. [20] And Adam gave names to all cattle, and to the fowl of the air, and to every beast of the field; but for Adam there was not found an help meet for him. [21] And the LORD God caused a deep sleep to fall upon Adam, and he slept: and he took one of his ribs, and closed up the flesh instead thereof; [22] And the rib, which the LORD God had taken from man, made he a woman, and brought her unto the man. [23] And Adam said, This is now bone of my bones, and flesh of my flesh: she shall be called Woman, because she was taken out of Man. [24] Therefore shall a man leave his father and his mother, and shall cleave unto his wife: and they shall be one flesh. [25] And they were both naked, the man and his wife, and were not ashamed.

In Genesis 2:25, the word "wife" is used, which therefore implies that a marriage took place. Adam never asked for a wife, but God saw how important it was for Adam to have a helper.

1.3 Identifying the husband

It is important now to identify the husband. Without first identifying the husband, it will be difficult to identify his roles.

Table 1. Identifying a man and a husband

Main components	Explanation
A man by birth	In the context of this literature and for simplicity's sake, a husband will be a man who was born as a man.
Marriage	The title of husband will be ascribed to a man who is committed to his female partner in marriage. Both of them have signed legal and religious documents to establish their marriage.
Has a wife	A man will only be considered a husband in this literature if he has a wife and continues his matrimonial duties. If his wife dies, then he is a widower. Wanting to be in multiple marriages will not allow a husband to be effective in his roles.

1.4 Children in the marriage

A man must not only be considered a husband if he has children with his wife, as some husbands may not want any children. Some women also do not want any children, and so their desire to marry has nothing to do with adding more members to their family.

In some marriages, one or both persons have children from previous relationships, and they may have determined that they do not want more children in this new marriage. There are other situations where the husband, wife, or both may not be able to contribute to the reproductive process. No one has complete control over their hormones except the Creator. Therefore, a couple's best effort to have children may not produce the intended results.

The story of Hannah and her husband is very familiar to many persons. They were married and wanted to have children, but the Lord had shut up Hannah's womb, so she had not conceived. Therefore, the best attempt by Hannah and Elkanah did not result in childbearing. However, Hannah vowed unto her God, and the Lord changed her situation from barrenness to being a mother.

1 Samuel 1:9-21

⁹ So Hannah rose up after they had eaten in Shiloh, and after they had drunk. Now Eli the priest sat upon a seat by a post of the temple of the LORD. ¹⁰ And she was in bitterness of soul, and prayed unto the LORD, and wept sore. ¹¹ And she vowed a vow, and said, O LORD of hosts, if thou wilt indeed look on the affliction of thine handmaid, and remember me, and not forget thine handmaid, but wilt give unto thine handmaid a man child, then I will give him unto the LORD all the days of his life, and there shall no razor come upon his head.

¹² And it came to pass, as she continued praying before the LORD, that Eli marked her mouth. ¹³ Now Hannah, she spake in her heart; only her lips moved, but her voice was not heard: therefore Eli thought she had been drunken. ¹⁴ And Eli said unto her, How long wilt thou be drunken? put away thy wine from thee. ¹⁵ And Hannah answered and said, No, my lord, I am a woman of a sorrowful spirit: I have drunk neither wine nor strong drink, but have poured out my soul before the LORD. ¹⁶ Count not thine handmaid for a daughter of Belial: for out of the abundance of my complaint and grief have I spoken hitherto. ¹⁷ Then Eli answered and said, Go in peace: and the God of Israel grant thee thy petition that thou hast asked of him. ¹⁸ And she said, Let thine handmaid find grace in thy sight. So the woman went her way, and did eat, and her countenance was no more sad.

¹⁹ And they rose up in the morning early, and worshipped before the LORD, and returned, and came to their house to Ramah: and Elkanah knew Hannah his wife; and the LORD remembered her. ²⁰ Wherefore it came to pass, when the time

was come about after Hannah had conceived, that she bare a son, and called his name Samuel, saying, Because I have asked him of the LORD. [21] And the man Elkanah, and all his house, went up to offer unto the LORD the yearly sacrifice, and his vow.

Some marriages will not produce children, but this does not stop a married man from being a husband or a married woman from being a wife.

1.5 Living together daily

Some husbands and wives will have employment that causes them to be away from their partners for lengthy periods of time. For example, some men may have to work in the hinterland or on a farm, and some women may have to travel to different communities and countries to execute their duties. Although they are not in the same house every day, this does not mean that they are not husband and wife. The most important thing for both of them is to remain committed to their marriage vows. They must respect each other and do nothing that could jeopardize their marriage.

In some marriages, one partner may only travel home to the family once per week or once per month. When they have those opportunities to be at home with their families, they have to continue to be that important person to their family, do the best they can, and then return to their work at the required time. It is often challenging when one partner has to spend much time away from the family, as it puts a strain on the other partner to take care of the family. Each partner needs to be loved and to communicate with their companion. Therefore, whenever it is possible for both persons to spend time together as a family, they must maximize those opportunities. When some persons marry, they may take a new job because they want to be closer to their family and spend more time with them. When children are part of the family, they often require the support and guidance of both parents.

1.6 Leaving one's parents and clinging to one's companion

There are some persons who are married but still want to enjoy the daily support of their parents. However, when an individual makes the choice to marry, they must be willing to leave their parents' house to go and live with their companion. As they spend more time together, they are expected to develop a better understanding of each other. Both persons in a marriage must learn to leave their parents and cleave to each other, as Jesus shared with the Pharisees.

Matthew 19:4-6

[4] And he answered and said unto them, Have ye not read, that he which made them at the beginning made them male and female, [5] And said, For this cause shall a man leave father and mother, and shall cleave to his wife: and they twain shall be one flesh? [6] Wherefore they are no more twain, but one flesh. What therefore God hath joined together, let not man put asunder.

2. Basic qualities of a husband

Husbands are expected to have the basic qualities discussed in this chapter. However, if they do not have all of these qualities, that does not disqualify them from being husbands. If a man was trained by parents who did not learn these qualities themselves, he might not embrace or practice these basic qualities. Other men possess more than these basic qualities when they get married.

2.1 A gentle person to his wife

It is expected that husbands will be gentle to their wives. They must treat their wives as an important resource in their marriages.

Colossians 3:19

[19] Husbands, love your wives, and be not bitter against them.

A husband must let his wife know that she is the queen in the marriage and that he is delighted to have her in his life. She must have that assurance that her husband, her king, is looking after her interests, and that he is in love with her alone.

Ephesians 5:25-29

[25] Husbands, love your wives, even as Christ also loved the church, and gave himself for it; [26] That he might sanctify and cleanse it with the washing of water by the word, [27] That he might present it to himself a glorious church, not having spot, or wrinkle, or any such thing; but that it should be holy and without blemish. [28] So ought men to love their wives as their own bodies. He that loveth his wife loveth himself. [29] For no man ever yet hated his own flesh; but nourisheth and cherisheth it, even as the Lord the church.

A husband must treat his wife well. She must not be treated as a slave in the marriage. A good husband will make his wife feel great, just like he wants to feel great.

2.2 Willing to take on challenges

Every marriage will have challenges, and not every husband will be able to adequately and independently address every problem that arises. Nevertheless, he must not run away from challenges. He must show his wife that he will stand up for the family, and that even when many things are not working the way the family expects, he will be there to work through those difficult challenges.

When husbands run away from challenges, they make their wives vulnerable. Some wives will look for other men who can stand up against challenges and be there for the family, and this situation may lead to a divorce because the wife needs a husband who is not afraid of challenges. However, while every marriage will go through many trials, those trials often make the marriage stronger and cause both persons to work as a team to succeed.

2.3 Loving toward his family and his wife's family

Every husband must have a love for his family. He must love his wife and their children, and he is also expected to love his extended family. When some men marry, they are only focused on their wives and forget her relatives, but they must love their wives' families and be supportive whenever the need arises. For both husbands and wives, it is difficult to love one's companion but hate their family.

Both persons in a marriage must be willing to visit each other's families. While they may not be able to make these visits regularly, they must plan some trips to be with family members. They can also arrange for family members to visit them. These opportunities to get together are expected to strengthen the relationship.

2.4 Showing love for people

A husband is expected to have a love for people. While he is not expected to love everyone, he also is not expected to hate everyone. However, if he hates people, he may soon begin to hate his companion and offspring. Hatred can be intense and hurtful to many persons. Therefore, husbands must show love to everyone, even when others are not loving them in return.

Wives will often have friends from before they were married, such as fellow students or even workmates. Husbands will also have childhood friends and workmates, and if they attend church or go to the markets, then there will be people for them to build friendships with. It would be very strange if those husbands cannot find a few persons to love and share friendship with. In some relationships, the wife's friends are also friends with the husband, and vice versa.

2.5 Trustworthy

A husband must be a trustworthy person. As he moves from singleness to married life, he must trust his partner, and if he shows that he is trustworthy, his partner will trust him.

When there is trust in the relationship, both partners feel comfortable sharing their feelings. They can laugh and cry about various matters without being afraid that whatever is done and said in secret will be revealed by their partner. Trustworthy persons do not always need too many details from their partners, such as a step-by-step account when they say they are going to visit their family. But when trust is lost in the relationship, there is little that one partner can do without the other partner being suspicious that something dishonest is being done.

Sometimes, one partner will search through the other partner's phone or documents to find private and personal information. When either or both persons take this approach, it indicates that they have not trusted each other, or that something wrong was done that needs to be investigated. This can be a dangerous position for each partner to be in.

2.6 Confidential

Confidentiality can be a big challenge for many marriages, as there will be many secret and private things said and done in the marriage. Both partners are expected to know many things about each other but not disclose certain information to anyone else.

Believers are expected to care for each other and to pray for each other when they are having problems. The burden of one believer must be the burden of another as they take the burden to the Lord. However, believers are not expected to disclose these burdens to strangers. The same thing is expected in a marriage: husbands and wives must care for each other but not disclose their problems to others.

Galatians 6:2

[2] Bear ye one another's burdens, and so fulfil the law of Christ.

When a wife is angry, she may say hurtful words, and her husband may be frustrated. When there are disagreements, however, he must not use that private and secret information to harm the marriage.

Any partner who likes to be a talebearer will hurt the relationship. They must not talk about their partner's private information with their parents or siblings, since this will harm their own relationship.

Proverbs 11:13

[13] A talebearer revealeth secrets: but he that is of a faithful spirit concealeth the matter.

Employees who occupy senior positions within organizations must sign confidentiality agreements. This is necessary because they will have access to information that must not be disclosed to others, and they are expected not to use this information to their own advantage. While couples are not required to sign confidentiality agreements, they must not disclose their private information to others unless they both agree to seek counseling or legal protection.

James 5:16

> [16] Confess your faults one to another, and pray one for another, that ye may be healed. The effectual fervent prayer of a righteous man availeth much.

Each partner must be able to disclose certain information with the other partner. However, some matters must be prayed about in private and not become a major news item.

2.7 A role model

Not all husbands will be perfect role models, but they must strive to be good role models. They must remember that whatever they do or say will impact their marriages. The things a husband says and does will have long-lasting impacts on their families, so they must guard against setting up their families for bad publicity.

Some wives choose to stay home or refuse to go somewhere with their husbands because of the poor reputations their husbands have caused for the family. It is embarrassing for wives and children to go places and hear about the bad things done by their husbands and fathers.

Matthew 5:16

> [16] Let your light so shine before men, that they may see your good works, and glorify your Father which is in heaven.

Christian husbands must be role models to their wives and children. People in the community must see them as good reflections of the family.

2.8 Committed to the marriage

A husband must demonstrate that he is committed to his marriage. If he does not have that commitment, the marriage will soon fall apart. He may even become committed to someone outside of the marriage, which is unacceptable.

Commitment to the relationship may be difficult at times, but husbands must remain committed. A husband must see his commitment to his marriage as more important than his commitment to his employer or the sports he loves.

When husbands are committed to their wives, they will be happy to be in their wives' presence. Before many persons were married, they had much time to spend with friends and relatives, but when they are married, they are committed to their wives and children. This positive change is necessary in order for married persons to build their relationships with their new families.

2.9 Accept that his wife is not perfect

Not all wives may like this statement, but no wife is perfect. All wives will continue to strive towards being better, but they will still have some flaws. Therefore, when a man marries the woman of his heart, he cannot compare her with his mother or place her alongside his sisters. He must not compare her with anyone else, since she is imperfect yet unique. Instead, he must work with her imperfections and help her to become better. As a husband, he must see himself as a farmer who tries to cultivate his estate into one from which he will get the best output. The work that he has to do with his wife may be great, but he must choose to do good things to help her to improve. There are times when his work to cultivate her will be frustrating, but he must be diligent in helping her become a better wife. He will be required to invest in her, not only for the moment but for the rest of his life.

In the New Testament, Peter stated that wives are weaker vessels, so Christian husbands should already know that they have some work to do with their wives.

1 Peter 3:7

[7] Likewise, ye husbands, dwell with them according to knowledge, giving honour unto the wife, as unto the weaker vessel, and as being heirs together of the grace of life; that your prayers be not hindered.

Those who nurture their partners to become better individuals must be congratulated. Sometimes, after trying very hard, parents give up on helping their adult children. Still, when those children marry, they may show significant improvement because their partners work with them to help them become great persons.

When a husband accepts that his wife is not perfect, he will spend less time frustrating himself and her over things he cannot change. As he accepts her shortcomings, he should concentrate his energies on her strengths, not her weaknesses.

Section 2: The husband's main roles

Some Christian men are afraid to marry because of the responsibilities associated with being a husband. However, men must be willing to take on these challenges, as they are expected to be leaders. When husbands are afraid to provide leadership to their families, they may cause other family members to take on the roles that husbands are expected to do.

Even if the entire family is depressed, husbands must motivate them to fulfill their dreams and march towards their goals. Wives need the support of their husbands on many occasions. Therefore, husbands, be the best supporter that your wife needs.

Provider and protector are other roles that Christian husbands are expected to fulfill. The husband might not always be the primary provider in the home, but he must still contribute to the success of his family. As protectors, husbands must keep their wives and children safe.

It is not guaranteed that all husbands will talk as much as their wives. However, husbands must still be effective in verbal and non-verbal communication with their wives.

Husbands are expected to give advice and to have a strategy for their family. First, they must think about where they would like their family to be within the next five or ten years. Then, based on this strategic direction, husbands may have to make a significant investment for their family.

Wives often love when their husbands contribute to domestic activities. Children sometimes love to seek out their fathers to cook for them, clean the house, or shop for groceries. Therefore, husbands must know where to find the kitchen utensils and how to prepare their family's favorite meals.

Husbands are not expected to know everything about their wives, but they must spend some time studying their wives. Once they have learned more, they must do things to bring joy into the marriage. Every wife wants to know that she has a husband who is her lover alone. Therefore, he must respect her in both private and public places.

After giving birth to children, wives may lose some of the physical beauty they had when they first entered the marriage. However, there is hope, as their husbands can help them stay healthy and in shape. Together, they can both arrange to eat healthy meals and to exercise. As they exercise, they may be able to reduce extra weight.

Wives love to be celebrated. Therefore, husbands, honor your wives. Look for every possible occasion to celebrate her. Let her know that she is the only woman in your life and that you are willing to give your time, money, and effort to celebrate the queen of your life.

3. Leader

As a husband, a man must demonstrate leadership abilities. No one is born a natural leader; instead, persons will learn to become leaders over time.

Joshua was called by God to lead the people of Israel after the death of Moses. However, Joshua was also a husband, and he understood the importance of leading his family in the ways of the Lord. He was bold enough to speak on his family's behalf about his decision to serve the Lord (Joshua 25:15).

Joshua 24:13-28

[13] And I have given you a land for which ye did not labour, and cities which ye built not, and ye dwell in them; of the vineyards and olive yards which ye planted not do ye eat. [14] Now therefore fear the LORD, and serve him in sincerity and in truth: and put away the gods which your fathers served on the other side of the flood, and in Egypt; and serve ye the LORD. [15] And if it seem evil unto you to serve the LORD, choose you this day whom ye will serve; whether the gods which your fathers served that were on the other side of the flood, or the gods of the Amorites, in whose land ye dwell: but as for me and my house, we will serve the LORD. [16] And the people answered and said, God forbid that we should forsake the LORD, to serve other gods; [17] For the LORD our God, he it is that brought us up and our fathers out of the land of Egypt, from the house of bondage, and which did those great signs in our sight, and preserved us in all the way wherein we went, and among all the people through whom we passed: [18] And the LORD drove out from before us all the people, even the Amorites which dwelt

in the land: therefore will we also serve the LORD; for he is our God. [19] And Joshua said unto the people, Ye cannot serve the LORD: for he is an holy God; he is a jealous God; he will not forgive your transgressions nor your sins. [20] If ye forsake the LORD, and serve strange gods, then he will turn and do you hurt, and consume you, after that he hath done you good. [21] And the people said unto Joshua, Nay; but we will serve the LORD. [22] And Joshua said unto the people, Ye are witnesses against yourselves that ye have chosen you the LORD, to serve him. And they said, We are witnesses. [23] Now therefore put away, said he, the strange gods which are among you, and incline your heart unto the LORD God of Israel. [24] And the people said unto Joshua, The LORD our God will we serve, and his voice will we obey. [25] So Joshua made a covenant with the people that day, and set them a statute and an ordinance in Shechem. [26] And Joshua wrote these words in the book of the law of God, and took a great stone, and set it up there under an oak, that was by the sanctuary of the LORD. [27] And Joshua said unto all the people, Behold, this stone shall be a witness unto us; for it hath heard all the words of the LORD which he spake unto us: it shall be therefore a witness unto you, lest ye deny your God. [28] So Joshua let the people depart, every man unto his inheritance.

Many persons begin to learn leadership skills from an early age. Some parents will assign various tasks to their sons to do within the home because they want their sons to understand that they will be involved in leadership roles throughout their lives. As those boys become older and have their own families, they will demonstrate many of the things they learned from their parents.

When God called Abram to move to a new location, Abram was willing to follow the voice of the Lord. Very importantly, Abram took his wife with him to the place to which God had called him. He was a husband who led from in front and also saw the need to have his family alongside him (Genesis 12:1-9). Abram showed that he was a family man, since he took his wife and his nephew with him. When Christian husbands go places, they must not be ashamed to bring their companions with them.

Genesis 12:1-9

[1] Now the LORD had said unto Abram, Get thee out of thy country, and from thy kindred, and from thy father's house, unto a land that I will shew thee: [2] And I will make of thee a great nation, and I will bless thee, and make thy name great; and thou shalt be a blessing: [3] And I will bless them that bless thee, and curse him that curseth thee: and in thee shall all families of the earth be blessed. [4] So Abram departed, as the LORD had spoken unto him; and Lot went with him: and Abram was seventy and five years old when he departed out of Haran. [5] And Abram took Sarai his wife, and Lot his brother's son, and all their substance that they had gathered, and the souls that they had gotten in Haran; and they went forth to go into the land of Canaan; and into the land of Canaan they came. [6] And Abram passed through the land unto the place of Sichem, unto the plain of Moreh. And the Canaanite was then in the land. [7] And the LORD appeared unto Abram, and said, Unto thy seed will I give this land: and there builded he an altar unto the LORD, who appeared unto him. [8] And he removed from thence unto a mountain on the east of Bethel, and pitched his tent, having Bethel on the west, and Hai on the east: and there he builded an altar unto the LORD, and called upon the name of the LORD. [9] And Abram journeyed, going on still toward the south.

Wives are often delighted when their husbands demonstrate that they know how to lead. The husband may not be an effective leader in every marriage, but he must know something about leading.

Wives who occupy senior positions within organizations and societies may still allow their husbands to fulfill the role of leader within the family. Some husbands may be intimidated by their wives' status in society and not want to demonstrate family leadership. However, many wives are eager for their husbands to demonstrate that they are leaders, not just good followers. In cases where the husband is not skilled enough to provide guidance, he must rely on the wisdom of his wife and let her ideas flow. He must not be afraid of not knowing everything as the leader. Indeed, many leaders in organizations do not know everything. However, they surround themselves with persons who will provide them with the technical knowledge and experiences that will allow the organization to succeed.

3.1 Natural leader

Husbands must be able to lead in the natural areas identified in the table below. They do not have to be the wisest persons, but they must be leaders. Being the leader also does not mean that they are the boss. E. M. Kelly states, "Remember the difference between a boss and a leader. A boss says, 'Go'. A leader says, 'Let's go'!" (Hughes et al., 2015).

As wives look toward their husbands as leaders, they first need to understand the different types of leaders. Next, they must understand which kind of leadership their husbands demonstrate based on that knowledge. Finally, they ought to know how to operate with their husbands. No husband will have all the types of leadership characteristics. However, whatever type he demonstrates may be a good starting point to work with him and spend less time challenging him to become someone he is not.

Table 2. Types of Leaders

Type of leader	Some identifiable components
Charismatic	The charismatic leader's influence springs mainly from their personality. The difficulty with charismatic leadership is that few people possess the exceptional qualities required to transform those all

	around them into willing followers. Another issue is that personal qualities, traits, or leadership skills cannot be acquired by training. They can only be modified by it.
Traditional	The traditional leader's position is assured by birth. This is another category to which few people can aspire.
Situational	The situational leader's influence can only be effective by being in the right place at the right time. This kind of leadership is too temporary in nature to be of much value in a business.
Appointed	The appointed leader's influence arises directly out of their position. This is a bureaucratic type of leadership, where legitimate power springs from the nature and scope of the position within the hierarchy.
Functional	The functional leader secures their leadership position by what they do rather than by who they are. In other words, functional leaders adapt their behaviors to meet the competing needs of the situation.

(Extracted from Cole, 1993)

There is always much discussion about leaders and leadership as people share their views about who is the best leader. Likewise, there are often discussions about who should lead political parties. Success in winning elections often rests upon those identified as leaders. While some political parties may have good strategies, if their leaders do not show signs of executing those strategies successfully, those parties may not win the general and regional elections.

According to Hughes et al. (2015), "researchers have defined leadership in many different ways":

- The process by which an agent induces a subordinate to behave in the desired manner
- Directing and coordinating the work of group members
- An interpersonal relation with which others comply because they want to, not because they have to
- The process of influencing an organized group toward accomplishing its goals
- Actions that focus resources to create desirable opportunities
- Creating conditions for a team to be effective
- The ability to get results and to build teams (these represent the "what" and "how" of leadership)
- A complex form of social problem solving

3.2 Zeal to do great things

As a husband, a man is expected to have a zeal to do great things. Even when his family may become tired or not show the fortitude to make great things happen, the husband must run with the vision and direction of the family. Many things will distract the family, but the husband must avoid showing frustration so that the family can accomplish great things. There will always be obstacles in a marriage, but the husband must find the courage to navigate his family through their challenges and make it great.

3.3 Execute the vision

Some husbands, as leaders, are great planners. They know where the family wants to go within a few years, and they have already mapped out their strategies. However, sadly, some of these husbands sit on their hands after making the plans. They talk plenty but do little.

It was God who saw the need for Adam to have a wife. Adam was such a great planner that God loved him and decided to reward him with a wife. Adam had vision, such that when the Lord asked him to name the animals, that did not appear to be a difficult task for him.

Whatever names Adam gave to those animals, God agreed with his choices (Genesis 3:19-20).

Genesis 2:18-20

[18] And the LORD God said, It is not good that the man should be alone; I will make him an help meet for him. [19] And out of the ground the LORD God formed every beast of the field, and every fowl of the air; and brought them unto Adam to see what he would call them: and whatsoever Adam called every living creature, that was the name thereof. [20] And Adam gave names to all cattle, and to the fowl of the air, and to every beast of the field; but for Adam there was not found an help meet for him.

Each husband must be courageous enough to execute the family's plan. It will be hard work, but he cannot quit. For example, many couples may live in rented houses after getting married, but they may plan to purchase their own lands and then build their own homes within a specific time frame. The husband must not allow that important dream to die but constantly work towards executing it so that the family can have their own home.

3.4 Spiritual leader

Besides being natural leaders, husbands must also provide spiritual leadership to their families. This may seem strange to some husbands, even if they are believers, but they ought to take the lead in this important area of their families' lives.

Figure 1. Religious things for the family to do

(All figures developed by the author unless otherwise noted.)

3.4.1 Prayer

Christian husbands must encourage their families to pray. The frequency of prayer will vary from family to family, but many families pray because they have seen the effect of prayer. For example, when a family member celebrates their birthday, one or all members may pray for that person. When a family member has an examination, others in the family will pray for their success. If family members are seeking finances to purchase or construct their own house, they may meet together and pray.

As an upright father, Job sacrificed burnt offerings for his sons. This was a way of sanctifying his sons before the Lord, which is a great thing that Christian fathers must do.

Job 1:4-5

[4] And his sons went and feasted in their houses, every one his day; and sent and called for their three sisters to eat and to drink with them. [5] And it was so, when the days of their feasting were gone about, that Job sent and sanctified them, and rose up early in the morning, and offered burnt offerings according to the number of them all: for Job said, It may be that my sons

have sinned, and cursed God in their hearts. Thus did Job continually.

Prayer also protects families from the unseen. For some families, prayers guide what they want to do.

3.4.2 Fasting

Christian families may celebrate many religious ceremonies, and fasting may be required. Even if a family does not spend much time embracing spiritual activities throughout the year, they may set aside time to fast for a particular religious season because they believe their family will receive great victory.

Husbands who are believers must set the example within the home by fasting and encouraging the family to do the same. Fasting may be challenging for some persons at the beginning, but once they make the sacrifice and endure a few days of fasting, then they may be able to last for a week. When families are fasting, they will make adjustments to their meals. While many Christian women will fast, they often look for the support of their husbands in fasting.

3.4.3 Studying religious teachings

Studying religious teachings ought to be a regular practice for Christian families. The husband or wife may lead the family devotions and teach other family members about the faith they embrace. These religious teachings often cause family members to have a strong foundation in their faith.

It is important that the family come together and study God's Word. When studying the Word of God, they must include their children in this important time.

Deuteronomy 6:7-9

[7] And thou shalt teach them diligently unto thy children, and shalt talk of them when thou sittest in thine house, and when thou walkest by the way, and when thou liest down, and when thou risest up. [8] And thou shalt bind them for a sign upon thine

hand, and they shall be as frontlets between thine eyes. [9] And thou shalt write them upon the posts of thy house, and on thy gates.

3.4.4 Praising

Husbands do not have to be great praise leaders, but they must encourage and participate in praising the Creator as a family. As part of the family devotions, praise will be important before or after teaching religious information.

When husbands are involved in religious activities, it often causes the children to follow that example. Of course, not all husbands will be spiritual leaders, but they must not distract their families from enhancing their spiritual understanding.

Every Christian family must be involved in praising God. Husbands must not be ashamed to praise the Lord, and they must encourage their family to join them in praising the Lord.

Psalm 34:1-4

[1] I will bless the LORD at all times: his praise shall continually be in my mouth. [2] My soul shall make her boast in the LORD: the humble shall hear thereof, and be glad. [3] O magnify the LORD with me, and let us exalt his name together. [4] I sought the LORD, and he heard me, and delivered me from all my fears.

God has delivered many families from their fears. Therefore, they must continue to magnify his holy name. As they bow down to him and acknowledge that he is their maker, he will lift them up before people.

Psalm 95:6

[6] O come, let us worship and bow down: let us kneel before the LORD our maker.

4. Motivator

No matter what good planners a husband and wife are, every marriage will face challenges. When family members are demotivated, husbands are expected to provide motivation. It may not be the easiest thing to do, but he must give his family the hope that the current challenges will be over. Although he does not know when that will occur, he must be like the lit coal in the middle of the winter. Even as external situations may drain the family's energy, the husband must remain the champion in the family. Even when he is weak and battered, he must show grit to benefit his family.

For example, wives may have miscarriages and be distraught about it. They may have many questions that they know their husbands cannot answer, but they will express their frustrations. Husbands in these circumstances must empathize with their wives and still motivate them to trust that life is not over. "A motive is a need or a driving force within a person" (Cole, 1993). Husbands must encourage their wives until they overcome their difficulties.

4.1 Give his wife hope

Every wife needs hope. She needs to know that something great will happen to the family. The marriage may have many challenges, but she needs to know that with her husband, the family will still accomplish its plans. He must comfort his family that only God knows the future and that God is working all things for his own good.

Romans 8:28

[28] And we know that all things work together for good to them that love God, to them who are the called according to his purpose.

4.2 Make her laugh during the storm

The storms of life are many. Many marriages are shattered because of the size and frequency of these storms. However, when husbands are good motivators, they can make their wives laugh through the storms. A husband needs to know how to ease his wife's stress and make her feel that whatever she is going through will soon be over.

Many politicians have learned to motivate their supporters while the economy is going through turmoil. Employees still go to work even when the workload is challenging because their leaders motivate them to do their best for the organization. Many working wives still go to work after having difficult days because their husbands encourage them to be good employees.

4.3 Motivate her to be there for the children

Some children will cause many problems for their parents. Parents may become emotionally disturbed when their children cause embarrassment to the family. However, the husband must motivate his wife to remain focused and not spend all of her time and effort trying to fix the problems their children cause. In the home, husbands may play a significant role in redirecting and disciplining children when they deviate from family values. Husbands must set moral values for the family to follow.

Some wives are not working because their husbands have asked them to be the homemaker. As a wife looks after the family business and the children, she may become exhausted at times. Listening to multiple children who each have their own idiosyncrasies is not easy for any parent. Therefore, for the success of the family, it will be important for both parents to be involved in raising their children.

5. Supporter

One of the things that wives expect from their husbands is support. Wives sometimes know that they might not have done all of the right things, but they need help from their husbands, even in times of difficulty.

5.1 Support his wife

Husbands must learn to be their wives' most prominent supporters. If wives do not get support from their husbands, some of them may accept support from other men and fall for them. Therefore, this means that the husband must know about the things his wife wants to do and support her.

For example, some wives will start their own businesses or want to do so. For such a wife, the support of her husband may be the most important asset she needs to make the business successful.

Some wives may desire to continue their studies. When husbands recognize that their wives want to increase their academics, they ought to support them, because in doing so, they are helping the entire family. Even if the husband has to stay up late to help his wife while she is studying, it will act as a great motivator. A husband may also take his wife to classes and return to pick her up, knowing that the entire family will benefit from her achievement.

Christian wives may have the desire to spend time doing religious things. While a husband may not be very active in the religious works that his wife will pursue, he can still support her. For example, if the wife is mainly the one who conducts the family devotions, her husband must give her support.

The support from husbands must be more than lip service; they must do many things to make sure their wives can see and feel their support. A little moral support to a wife may be worth more than any money her husband can give to her.

Wives who are pregnant need all the support they can get from their husbands. On many occasions, wives will go through complications during their pregnancies, as shown in the table below, and they need their husbands to be at their side to provide encouraging words to them until the baby is delivered.

Table 3. Possible pregnancy complications and risk factors

A. The development of obstetrically related conditions during the pregnancy, such as vaginal bleeding, toxic states, and premature labor
B. Medical conditions such as cardiac disease, diabetes, or infection
C. Unfavorable obstetrical histories such as high parity – five or more pregnancies, previous infant death, premature birth, or infant with congenital malformations, difficulty in conceiving, less than a year since pregnancy, or Rh incompatibility and sensitization
D. Psychosocial conditions such as being under 17 years of age, narcotic or alcohol addiction, and poverty

(Extracted from Smith, 1988)

While not every wife will go through the complications listed in the table above, they will still need much support from their husbands during pregnancy. Husbands must take the time to attend a family clinic with their pregnant wives. They will better understand their wives' struggles as they ask the doctors their questions and hear what the doctors tell their wives. If wives recognize that their husbands will support them during and after pregnancy, they will be willing to have more children because they know the support is there.

5.2 Support the children

If the marriage has produced children, husbands must support them as well. While a man's support for the children must not be greater than his support for his wife, he must still support them.

Ephesians 6:4

4 And, ye fathers, provoke not your children to wrath: but bring them up in the nurture and admonition of the Lord.

One or both persons may enter a marriage with children from another union. A husband must support his children from his previous relationship or marriage, and he must also support his wife's children from before both of them became one.

When a woman recognizes that her companion does not adequately care for her children, she tends to operate differently, as women greatly value their children. Therefore, husbands, love your wives and the additional children in the relationship so that you can have enjoyable family time. Children often notice when they are not treated as family members but as outsiders, and this causes many children to be withdrawn.

If children have homework or assignments, husbands must also give their support. They can assist the children with their tasks by purchasing the required learning materials for them. Husbands must also stay up late with their children, if the need arises, to get some work completed while their wives rest.

Children may have to attend cultural activities and sports. In such cases, husbands can take the children to those activities and return to pick them up at the appropriate times. When husbands do these important duties, they often win their families' hearts. Husbands do not have to be millionaires to make their families happy, as their moral support will bring ease and joy to the family. When children see that their fathers are demonstrating love towards them, they tend to show appreciation to their fathers. Some fathers, when they are aged, wonder why their children are not supporting them, and it might be because they did not support their children during those early years of their lives.

5.3 Give support without any expectation

Husbands must give support to their wives without expecting anything in return. They must do this because they love their wives and know their own roles. Wives must understand that they can count on their husbands' support. A wife must boast among her friends that her husband will be there to support her. Wives must not do wrong things and expect their husbands to condone their destructive behavior: if they are wrong, they must be told that they are wrong. However, the correction must be done from a loving heart to help wives become better. For the husband to correct his wife, he must be leading an exemplary life pleasing in the sight of God.

As Jesus continued his teaching, he told believers to love each other and also to love their enemies. This means that family members must love each other even when something wrong has been done, and they must love without expecting anything in return.

Luke 6:27-36

[27] But I say unto you which hear, Love your enemies, do good to them which hate you, [28] Bless them that curse you, and pray for them which despitefully use you. [29] And unto him that smiteth thee on the one cheek offer also the other; and him that taketh away thy cloak forbid not to take thy coat also. [30] Give to every man that asketh of thee; and of him that taketh away thy goods ask them not again. [31] And as ye would that men should do to you, do ye also to them likewise. [32] For if ye love them which love you, what thank have ye? for sinners also love those that love them. [33] And if ye do good to them which

do good to you, what thank have ye? for sinners also do even the same. [34] And if ye lend to them of whom ye hope to receive, what thank have ye? for sinners also lend to sinners, to receive as much again. [35] But love ye your enemies, and do good, and lend, hoping for nothing again; and your reward shall be great, and ye shall be the children of the Highest: for he is kind unto the unthankful and to the evil. [36] Be ye therefore merciful, as your Father also is merciful.

6. Provider

Another important role for husbands to know and perform is that of the provider. This does not mean that the husband has to be working for the most money in the marriage, but he must contribute financially. If a husband is not working for a large remuneration when he first marries his wife, he must seek opportunities to earn more for the benefit of his family. When a man is single, he may live on meager wages, but his earnings need to increase when he has a wife and children. If the wife is more qualified and marketable than the husband, the husband still remains the head of the home and must be allowed to make prudent financial decisions in the family.

Christian husbands must be mindful that they do not bring the faith into disrepute. They are expected to make a great effort to provide for their families, even if they are not working for much money.

1 Timothy 5:8

[8] But if any provide not for his own, and specially for those of his own house, he hath denied the faith, and is worse than an infidel.

6.1 Provider to his wife

Husbands must be providers to their wives. Even when wives are earning, and perhaps even earning more than their husbands, they must offer some financial contribution to their wives. Although a wife may know that her husband makes less money than she does, she knows her husband is making an important sacrifice. As men give money and gifts to their wives, they are expressing love, care, and appreciation, and this solidifies the marriage.

God only brought Eve into the life of Adam after first proving that Adam was a hard worker who would be able to provide for his wife (Genesis 2:18-25). Jacob worked hard for his father-in-law, Laban, before he could get Rachel to be his wife. It is often seen that men must be employed before considering marriage, since they are expected to provide for their families.

Genesis 29:16-21

16 And Laban had two daughters: the name of the elder was Leah, and the name of the younger was Rachel. 17 Leah was tender eyed; but Rachel was beautiful and well favoured. 18 And Jacob loved Rachel; and said, I will serve thee seven years for Rachel thy younger daughter. 19 And Laban said, It is better that I give her to thee, than that I should give her to another man: abide with me. 20 And Jacob served seven years for Rachel; and they seemed unto him but a few days, for the love he had to her. 21 And Jacob said unto Laban, Give me my wife, for my days are fulfilled, that I may go in unto her.

6.2 Sharing family expenses

Sometimes, one partner's income may not be sufficient to maintain the family. Therefore, both partners will have to share the family expenses. Even in cases where the wife is working for more than her husband, the husband must take one or more expenses that he will faithfully pay when due.

In some marriages, one partner may be better than the other at managing the family's finances. Therefore, whoever is more suited to this responsibility should be given opportunities to earn and pay the family's expenses. Many families will have major costs that they have to pay, some of which must be paid monthly, such as mortgages and vehicle loans.

6.3 Provider to his children

Husbands must also provide for their children. Children will need new clothes, and when they are attending school, they will need school supplies. Sometimes, the transportation cost for children to get to and from school may represent a significant amount of their parents' earnings.

The Bible reminds persons in Psalm 127:3 that children are an inheritance of the lord. Therefore, parents must provide for God's inheritance.

Psalm 127:3-5

³ Lo, children are an heritage of the LORD: and the fruit of the womb is his reward. ⁴ As arrows are in the hand of a mighty man; so are children of the youth. ⁵ Happy is the man that hath his quiver full of them: they shall not be ashamed, but they shall speak with the enemies in the gate.

Parents must seek to provide their children with a stipend to settle the family expenses, as children like to know that they have money to spend on their parents. However, parents must teach their children to use their stipends wisely. The amount of money given to them must not be lavish, even if parents can afford to give large sums. Parents must also teach their children to save some of the funds they receive. When children learn to save, they may take the same practice into their adult lives.

Every husband must challenge himself to provide for his family and leave an inheritance for them. Therefore, when men are considering entering a relationship, they must carefully think about providing not just for their wives alone, but also for any children they may have together.

Proverbs 13:22

²² A good man leaveth an inheritance to his children's children: and the wealth of the sinner is laid up for the just.

6.4 Other ways of meeting the family's needs

A husband might not provide financially for his wife every day. However, he can contribute other things that are important to the marriage. For example, if he is a farmer, he will provide some of the produce from the farm, which can include meats and animal-related produce, as well as vegetables and fruits. These products from the family farm have costs attached to them, but when they are provided to the family, the family does not have to spend money to purchase them.

If a husband is a mason or carpenter, he can use his skills and knowledge to help his family when they are ready to build their own house. While he will not expect payment for his labor and skills, the cost of constructing the house will be lower because of his contributions. It may take several months, or even years, to complete the construction of the house. However, if he gives his labor to this important investment of the family, then he will reduce the overall costs for the finished product.

Similarly, a husband who operates his own cab service may transport his family members. If he can do this regularly, he will be contributing to his family.

6.5 Establishing savings

Husbands must work along with their families to have some amount of money saved. Sometimes, at the initial stage of the marriage, the family may be unable to save any money, because they have to care for their children and probably repay a loan or mortgage. However, the family must take advantage of any opportunities to establish a savings account.

There will always be family emergencies. Some emergencies may not be expensive, but others, such as accidents, may be costly to the family. One accident may require family members to find a great sum of money to repair their vehicle or the other person's vehicle.

In the case of sickness, no one knows when their health will fail them. However, if they have savings, they can use some of those funds to settle their medical expenses. Once those emergency medical expenses are settled, the family can return to saving money.

Both husband and wife must be disciplined whenever they plan to save money. There will always be things they think they would like to have, but those things may not all be critical. A disciplined family managing their finances can accomplish more than many persons who earn more money than they do.

Every dollar saved in the marriage can be used for further investment in the family. Even the groceries they purchase may be able to be reduced without compromising the family's health. If the husband is not the greater financial contributor in the home, he must seek other ways to provide for the family or save money.

6.6 Give good gifts to the children

Fathers are reminded in Matthew 7:9-11 to listen to the needs of their children and give them good gifts. Yes, there are times when children feel as if their parents own everything and, as a result, will often ask for whatever they want. Children will continue to ask for many things, but fathers must know what is best to give to their children.

Matthew 7:9-11

[9] Or what man is there of you, whom if his son ask bread, will he give him a stone? [10] Or if he ask a fish, will he give him a serpent? [11] If ye then, being evil, know how to give good gifts unto your children, how much more shall your Father which is in heaven give good things to them that ask him?

7. Protector

The reason some women marry is that they need a protector in their lives. While many women can purchase security cameras or even have a firearm, there is an additional level of comfort that they have when they are married to a man.

Some wives like to sleep in the arms of their husbands because it makes them feel protected. When they go to the market, they may take their husband with them as a defensive presence. The physical size of a husband does not determine his ability to protect his wife.

7.1 Protector for his wife

One main role that wives expect from their husbands is that of the protector. The figure below identifies several types of protection that many husbands offer to their wives.

Figure 2. Types of protection husbands can offer to their wives

7.1.1 Physical protection

There are times when husbands will have to defend their wives physically. For example, in the case of a robbery, the presence and response of a husband can scare off would-be bandits. Sometimes, when bandits are planning to commit illegal acts, they see single women as vulnerable but see married women as being protected. When neighbors threaten to harm each other, husbands will have to be there to protect their wives. In some families, parents and siblings may want to harm a daughter who has left them to marry, so her husband will have to physically protect her against her own parents and siblings.

When Nehemiah was rebuilding the wall, he knew that intruders wanted to invade the place and take the people as captives. However, Nehemiah commanded the men to continue building the wall and be watchful. He even made it clear that they must be watchful for their families, including their wives.

Nehemiah 4:13-15

[13] Therefore set I in the lower places behind the wall, and on the higher places, I even set the people after their families with their swords, their spears, and their bows. [14] And I looked, and rose up, and said unto the nobles, and to the rulers, and to the rest of the people, Be not ye afraid of them: remember the LORD, which is great and terrible, and fight for your brethren, your sons, and your daughters, your wives, and your houses. [15] And it came to pass, when our enemies heard that it was known unto us, and God had brought their counsel to nought, that we returned all of us to the wall, every one unto his work.

In another example from the Old Testament, Pharaoh wanted to kill Moses because Moses had killed an Egyptian. However, Moses fled to Midian, a strange land. As Moses was at the well, Reuel's daughters came there to draw water to give to the sheep. While they were there, some shepherds came and drove them away. Moses had no relationship with Reuel or his daughters, but he hated the injustice, so he defended Reuel's daughters against the shepherds. When Reuel heard that his daughters had been rescued by a strange man, he inquired about this stranger. As a father, he was delighted that there was someone who provided protection to his daughters. He rewarded Moses for his protection over his daughters' lives by giving him Zipporah to marry. This ought to be an important lesson to men, whether they are husbands or not, that they must be there to protect their wives and other women.

Exodus 2:15-21

[15] Now when Pharaoh heard this thing, he sought to slay Moses. But Moses fled from the face of Pharaoh, and dwelt in the land of Midian: and he sat down by a well. [16] Now the priest of Midian had seven daughters: and they came and drew water, and filled the troughs to water their father's flock. [17] And the shepherds came and drove them away: but Moses stood up and helped them, and watered their flock. [18] And when they came to Reuel their father, he said, How is it that ye are come so soon to day? [19] And they said, An Egyptian delivered us out of the hand of the shepherds, and also drew water enough for us, and watered the flock. [20] And he said unto his daughters, And where is he? why is it that ye have left the man? call him, that he may eat bread. [21] And Moses was content to dwell with the man: and he gave Moses Zipporah his daughter.

7.1.2 Emotional protection

Wives go through so many emotional challenges, and they should be comforted by their husbands during these challenges. Through the mere fact that he is with her at home, a wife may feel more emotionally relaxed. If a wife experiences difficult days at work, her husband can provide emotional protection. Husbands must listen to their wives whenever they are depressed and offer them hope.

Wives can sometimes experience verbal abuse from their employers, but if their husbands intervene on their behalf, such abuse will cease. Some husbands will declare that nobody will trouble their wives or cause them emotional trauma.

7.1.3 Financial protection

The money some women earn may not be adequate to take care of most of their needs. Therefore, when they are married and their husbands contribute financially, it provides additional resources to their lives.

When a husband is unable to protect his family financially, he causes embarrassment for the family. If he were to die suddenly, it could change his family's life and even cause them to become slaves to people in order to repay any outstanding debts.

2 Kings 4:1-2

[1]Now there cried a certain woman of the wives of the sons of the prophets unto Elisha, saying, Thy servant my husband is dead; and thou knowest that thy servant did fear the LORD: and the creditor is come to take unto him my two sons to be bondmen. [2]And Elisha said unto her, What shall I do for thee? tell me, what hast thou in the house? And she said, Thine handmaid hath not any thing in the house, save a pot of oil.

The prophet Elisha came to this widow's rescue. He told her what to do, and when she followed the instructions of God's servant, she was able to repay her creditors and keep her sons.

Some women may want to pursue higher education but do not have the financial resources. However, if they have a companion, they may receive additional finances from that person to complete their studies. Some women living in rented houses or in their parents' homes may want to move into their own house, and this dream may be realized when they get married.

When wives have financial transactions to complete, they may need their husbands to be there with them. For example, if a wife is purchasing a vehicle, she may ask her husband to accompany her because she knows that he is a good negotiator and may be more knowledgeable about vehicles, and he may also be vigilant so that that no one attempts to swindle his wife out of her money.

7.1.4 Spiritual protection

Husbands who have a religious background and practice religious teachings will also provide spiritual protection for their wives. Of course, there are evil spirits, but the prayer of a Christian husband will drive those evil spirits away.

Some women looking for a man to marry want to find someone who practices the same religion. When this happens, these women know that they will get spiritual protection from their husbands, who will intercede on their behalf.

Many wives feel comfortable and protected during family devotions when their husbands are involved. They believe that he provides spiritual headship to the family and that they can rely on him to lead the family spiritually.

1 Corinthians 11:3

³ But I would have you know, that the head of every man is Christ; and the head of the woman is the man; and the head of Christ is God.

Ephesians 5:25

²⁵ Husbands, love your wives, even as Christ also loved the church, and gave himself for it.

7.2 Protector of his children

Husbands must also protect their children. Children sometimes boast that their fathers will defend them. If they are being bullied at school, they often complain to their fathers because they want to be protected from bullies. Children may be afraid of dogs and other animals, but when they are with their fathers, they feel protected.

7.3 Protector of the family's possessions

Every family will have possessions, though the amount and types will vary from family to family. For example, families may have houses, vehicles, land, furniture, and electrical appliances. Wives will expect their husbands to protect these family possessions. A husband does not have to be the most muscular man on the planet, as his mere presence will be enough to act as security for the family's possessions.

In some homes, the husband will make sure to lock the house properly before going to bed if all the family members are at home. He will walk around the house before bed and ensure that all windows and doors are properly secured. He will also ensure that the home's security lights are on during the evening. If the family has dogs, the husband may ensure that the dogs are loosed to guard and protect the family possessions in the night.

In cases where the husband will have to be away from the homes for extended periods, he may acquire closed-circuit surveillance for his family. This will ensure that the family can see if anyone is illegally trying to enter the home or remove any of the family's possessions.

Husbands who are working may place insurance coverage on the house and any family vehicles, so that if anything happens, the family is protected and will be compensated for any losses suffered.

8. Communicator

A husband must be a good communicators with his wife. However, being a good communicator does not mean that he has to be talking all the time. While husbands may like talking, they may not match word for word with their wives. Marriage is never about competition but about complementing each other.

8.1 Good listener

A husband is expected to practice excellent communication with his wife, and he must learn to listen as she communicates with him. In addition, he will have to train himself to listen to her, especially if he is not accustomed to spending time with women and receiving guidance from them.

Figure 3. Verbal and non-verbal communication is important for husbands to know about their wives

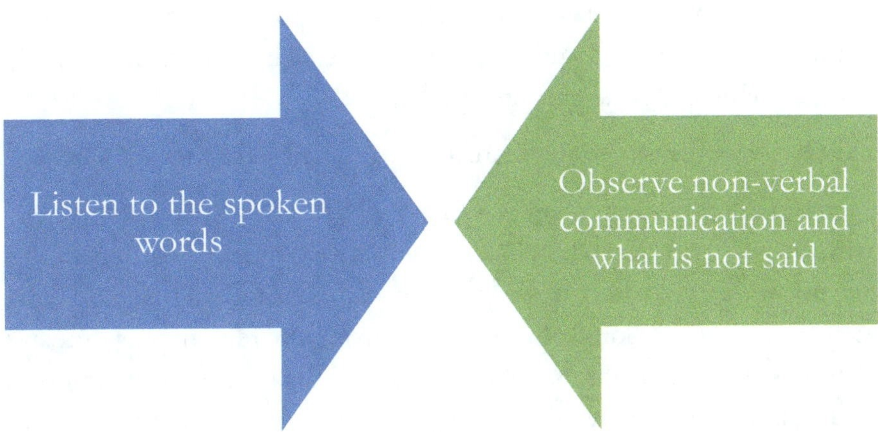

There are disagreements in every relationship, but both partners must learn to work as a team. The Apostle James reminds believers to be quick to hear and slow to anger. It is very important that both partners be willing to communicate. If they are going to be effective in their communication, they must be willing to listen to each other.

James 1:19-20

[19] Wherefore, my beloved brethren, let every man be swift to hear, slow to speak, slow to wrath: [20] For the wrath of man worketh not the righteousness of God.

8.2 Listen to the spoken words

On many occasions, wives will talk about whatever is affecting them. However, if a wife is constantly telling her husband about the same thing, he can become tired of hearing the same topic or complaint. Nevertheless, she may only be sharing the same views repeatedly because he did not take the necessary action in the first place.

Many wives prefer to talk about private matters with their husbands when they are alone, such as in the bedroom or traveling together in their private vehicle. Husbands need to understand when their wives are just providing them with basic information to observe. But there are other times when wives offer critical information that their husbands must listen to and take action. For example, many wives have eyes to see when other women may be trying to invade their marriage and will warn their husbands to put an end to all intruders. Love should not be polluted by casual friendships.

8.3 Observe non-verbal communication and what is not said

Non-verbal communication is a big area that some husbands struggle with. A husband may often listen to his wife's spoken words, but not always understand her message when she has not said a word. For example, a specific kind of eye contact from a wife may speak greater volumes than all the words she would like to say. Gentle eye contact with a smiling face may be a message telling a husband to get closer to his wife. However, if she has a severe face and gives a stern look, she may be sending a message that she does not approve of something her husband are doing, and that he must stop whatever he is doing or keep his distance.

As the marriage grows older, husbands are expected to understand and interpret their wives' non-verbal communication. Unfortunately, there is no university they can attend to help them interpret the messages their wives will send to them. They will have many days of trial and error, but they must show signs of improving their ability to understand their wives.

8.4 Talker

Not every husband likes to talk. However, husbands cannot operate like silent monuments in the marriage. Every husband is blessed with a voice, and he must be able to express himself in his own way. Even if their wives are brilliant, husbands must find ways to convey their spoken words to them. If a man has married a woman who is very educated and he is not at the same level, then it may be a reason for him to consider increasing his knowledge. Nevertheless, a marriage is never about a competition of knowledge. What may be most important is for the husband to find things to talk about with his wife.

Strangely, it may be the case that during the time of courtship, both persons were very verbose, but after getting married, it appears as if their speech was taken from them. However, as men keep talking to their wives, they allow their wives to understand them and their thinking.

Figure 4. Why husbands need to be good communicators in their marriage

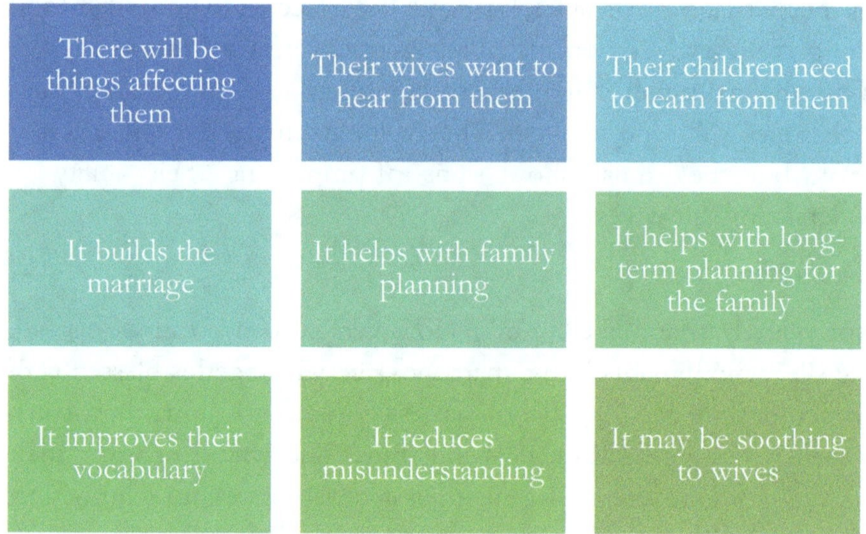

8.4.1 There will be things affecting them

Some persons think that only women are affected by things, and only women have issues. However, men are humans and are also affected by many things. For example, husbands may have hard days at work that they need to talk about. If they have aggressive employers, this may affect their thinking and make them feel insignificant.

Husbands will have health issues, and there are times when they will want to discuss those matters first with their wives. Sometimes, as they share their health issues, their wives may provide solutions. Some wives will visit the health institutions with their husbands whenever they have to go there for any medical issue. With some health issues, wives can make changes to the meals they prepare to allow their husbands to live long and healthy lives. Some wives will go with their husbands to support them as they exercise, restoring their health. Whatever support a husband can receive from his wife will always add great value to the marriage.

Some husbands are very honest and will tell their wives about other women showing interest in them. Many wives will provide sound advice to their husbands about what they must do to prevent extramarital affairs. Husbands need to listen to that advice and stay away from any infidelity.

8.4.2 Their wives want to hear from them

Husbands must know that their wives want to hear from them. Therefore, they must open their mouths and say something to their wives, even just to have a jovial conversation. Wives like to know about the things that are affecting their husbands, as well as the things that make their husbands happy.

Husbands should not pass information through their children to their wives; they must have direct conversations. When one parent goes through their children to communicate with the other parent, it often creates many conflicts in the marriage.

Some wives may not know about their husbands' childhood days and hope that he will share some of that important history as they talk frequently. Many persons are influenced by their childhood even today. Therefore, when husbands speak of their past, they help their wives to know more about them. She may treat him differently, since she now understands why her husband was behaving differently in the past.

8.4.3 Their children need to learn from them

Children sometimes spend much time with their mothers because their fathers do not say too much. When some fathers open their mouths to speak, it is often to correct or discipline their children. Children need to have good conversations with their fathers, and their fathers must motivate them to become great persons.

When children have school assignments, they must be comfortable going to their fathers to get answers and guidance. Likewise, when young adults think about finding companions, they must discuss those matters with their fathers and receive proper advice.

8.4.4 It builds the marriage

When husbands talk, it builds the marriage, as it allows both persons to learn more about each other. They can agree and disagree but still find an amicable solution to their concerns. More husbands must take the liberty of being involved in more conversations within the family. Even when husbands and wives are watching movies together, husbands must be willing to share their views, as their wives may say things to try to get their opinion on what they are watching. As husband and wife travel together in their private transportation, they have more time to talk. If they go to the market and supermarket together, they can continue many conversations.

There are times when wives just want to hear from their husbands. For example, if the husband is working and his wife is at home, she will often ask him, "How was your day at work?" This simple question can lead to a long conversation, which may be very important for the marriage.

8.4.5 It helps with family planning

Both husband and wife must discuss family planning. It must not be thought of as a secret thing. As they discuss this important matter together, they will decide how to take care of their family as they work towards accomplishing their dreams and aspirations.

In family planning, they can discuss and agree on what method of contraception will be most appropriate. However, they must be open about this important aspect of their lives, since many of their long-term plans may not be realized if they cannot plan how many children they would like to have and when.

Table 4. Advantages and disadvantages of the main methods of contraception

Method	Advantages and disadvantages
Abstention	Completely effective but relies on the self-control of both partners.
Withdrawal	Very unreliable; relies on self-control of both partners.
Rhythm method	It is not reliable; it can be effective if the woman has regular periods and keeps careful dates.
Condoms	It is very effective if used carefully, but couples need to have them at hand. This is because they are also important in preventing transmission of infection.
Combined pill	Very effective, provided the woman doesn't forget to take it each day; often reduces pains; can cause high blood pressure or other medical conditions in some women.
Progestogen-only pill	Very effective, provided the woman doesn't forget to take it each day at the same time.
Intra-uterine device	Very effective; needs to be fitted by a doctor.
Diaphragm	Very effective; needs to be inserted before sexual intercourse and removed about six hours later; needs to be obtained from a doctor or family planning clinic.

Male sterilization (vasectomy)	Very effective; only needs to be done once and usually irreversible.
Female sterilization	Very effective; only needs to be done once and usually irreversible.

(Extracted from Givens et al., 2010)

The methods of contraception must be discussed and agreed upon by both persons. This important discussion will reduce conflicts when they engage in sexual intercourse.

8.4.6 It helps with long-term planning for the family

Every family must plan for the future, since today will soon be over. As husbands and wives talk, they will share some of their long-term goals with one another. They may then establish timelines for those goals, and every year they will review how many of those goals they have accomplished.

If a family wants to construct a house, both husband and wife must have an input. The design and cost of the home must not be left to the person who earns the most money; rather, both persons must be involved in the decision-making.

To purchase a family vehicle, both partners must first discuss this matter. They must carefully consider the cost of the car. If the family is large, they must also consider what size vehicle will meet the family's needs, and they should also discuss and agree on the color of the vehicle.

8.4.7 It improves their vocabulary

Many husbands do not like talking much. However, they must know that when they engage in many conversations, they give themselves more opportunities to increase their vocabulary. So, while some husbands may not like to talk very much, their vocabulary improves through having discussions.

When fathers have to attend school meetings on behalf of their children, they must be in sync with the verbal discussion so that they can represent their families. If husbands have their proper place and represent the family, they must do so reasonably. Some husbands will avoid talking to represent the family at wedding receptions and funeral services. They do not want to talk because they are afraid that they do not know what to say, or that they may say the wrong things. However, if husbands practice speaking regularly within their family circle, they will become better whenever they talk on their family's behalf.

8.4.8 It reduces misunderstanding

If a husband does not always verbally express himself, his wife have to assume what he would like to say or may be thinking, which can lead to misunderstandings. However, when husbands verbally express themselves, they reduce the possibility of their wives assuming what they are thinking. Children may go to their mothers more often because mothers often talk more, so the children believe that their mothers know everything. However, children also love to hear from their fathers.

Husbands will experience many challenges and may be quiet at home as they internalize certain matters. However, when they express themselves, their family will understand what is affecting them and can try to help them.

8.4.9 It may be soothing to wives

When a wife wants to hear someone speaking to her, the best person to do so ought to be her husband. Some wives will have regular conversations with their mothers because they just want someone to talk to. Conversations between mothers and daughters may continually repeat the same information, but they find this soothing. Therefore, husbands must learn to talk with their wives as well. It may take time, but if they start to make deliberate efforts, they will soon become better at having long and regular conversations with their wives.

Sadly, it is seen that some women will become victims to certain men because of the charming words they utter. For example, a wife may be in a good marriage and have most of the resources she needs, but when some strange man keeps speaking to her and telling her what she wants to hear, she can become the victim of an extramarital affair.

Husbands, you have significant work to do. First, start talking with your wife. You are not in a classroom where your conversations always have to be perfect. Just talk and see how she responds. After some months or years of talking with her, you may come to know the types of conversations your wife likes. Now and again, let your conversation send the message that you are a romantic husband who is interested in her. Your wife must hear from you that you love her. Tell this to her as often as possible, so that if any other man tries to say soothing words to her, it will not mean anything because she has heard you say these words so many times.

8.5 Non-verbal communication

Husbands must also learn that they do not always have to talk for their wives to understand them. They must also utilize non-verbal communication to gain their wives' attention. For example, eye contact from a husband can send a good message to his wife, and the way he dresses or the fragrance he wears can also communicate his intentions and mood to her.

Husbands must be diplomatic in conveying messages to their companions. The very touch from a husband may make his wife emotional, so he has to know when and where to touch her.

A fresh shave and haircut can convey an intentional message from a husband. Some husbands may wear certain clothes at home to form a closer bond with their wives. When husbands celebrate their wives' birthdays, the selection and value of gifts may also be good non-verbal communicators.

When husbands hold their wives' hands in gentle ways, this may generate positive emotional responses. A husband purchasing particular clothes for his wife that she likes may also send positive messages. If husbands serve their wives breakfast in bed, then collect and wash the dirty utensils, these actions may communicate so much to wives that they have caring husbands.

8.6 Tell her kind words

Husbands cannot be afraid to tell their wives kind words. They ought to do this frequently, since many wives like to hear kind words. King Solomon provided an example for husbands to follow.

Song of Solomon 1:1-17

[1] The song of songs, which is Solomon's. [2] Let him kiss me with the kisses of his mouth: for thy love is better than wine. [3] Because of the savour of thy good ointments thy name is as ointment poured forth, therefore do the virgins love thee. [4] Draw me, we will run after thee: the king hath brought me into his chambers: we will be glad and rejoice in thee, we will remember thy love more than wine: the upright love thee. [5] I am black, but comely, O ye daughters of Jerusalem, as the tents of Kedar, as the curtains of Solomon. [6] Look not upon me, because I am black, because the sun hath looked upon me: my mother's children were angry with me; they made me the keeper of the vineyards; but mine own vineyard have I not kept. [7] Tell me, O thou whom my soul loveth, where thou feedest, where thou makest thy flock to rest at noon: for why should I be as one that turneth aside by the flocks of thy companions?

[8] If thou know not, O thou fairest among women, go thy way forth by the footsteps of the flock, and feed thy kids beside the shepherds' tents. [9] I have compared thee, O my love, to a company of horses in Pharaoh's chariots. [10] Thy cheeks are comely with rows of jewels, thy neck with chains of gold. [11] We will make thee borders of gold with studs of silver.

[12] While the king sitteth at his table, my spikenard sendeth forth the smell thereof. [13] A bundle of myrrh is my well-beloved unto me; he shall lie all night betwixt my breasts. [14] My beloved is unto me as a cluster of camphire in the vineyards of Engedi.

[15] Behold, thou art fair, my love; behold, thou art fair; thou hast doves' eyes.

[16] Behold, thou art fair, my beloved, yea, pleasant: also our bed is green.

[17] The beams of our house are cedar, and our rafters of fir.

These kind words often mean so much to wives. It can make their day or make them feel romantic.

9. Advisor and strategist

Husbands must be seen for more than their physical bodies: they must be seen as men who put their brains to great use. Wives enjoy husbands who have a vision. Such husbands know what they would like to see happen for their families beyond today, and they share those plans with their wives.

9.1 Critical thinker

Not everything that happens in the family can be addressed with ordinary thinking. There are times when critical thinking will be needed, and husbands must show that they are made of the right material to think critically.

Thinking critically does not always require attending a higher level of education. Some husbands have not received much formal training, but they are still able to think critically.

Critical thinkers often remove emotions from their thinking and work with facts. They do not allow their minds to blur what is happening immediately, since they are thinking several days or even months ahead.

Those who aspire to be critical thinkers must gather facts. Then, based upon the facts, they will make prudent decisions and try to live by the decisions they make. A critical thinker will need up-to-date and regular information, so they may listen to daily news and attend important events to get good information to help their families.

Wives often feel comfortable knowing that their husbands are not living only for today and that they can see the bigger picture in life. These husbands know that they are not competing with other husbands, but they are doing their best to protect and provide for their families.

Many critical thinkers are not afraid to take on challenges, and they often look for opportunities to prove that they can make something great happen. For example, some critical thinkers may be from families that lived in poverty in previous generations, but they have challenged themselves that their new family will not live in poverty. Therefore, they will think of ways for their families to live successful and prosperous lives.

9.2 Long-term planner

Husbands must also be involved in long-term planning. Family planning is one such area where long-term planning is needed. Additionally, both wife and husband must determine what assets they need to acquire. For example, they may plan to own their own vehicles within the first five years after their wedding and to have their own house within the first ten years. This is an important reason why both husband and wife must have regular conversations. It may be difficult for one family member to acquire these assets alone, so they will have to put their resources together to accomplish these goals. Therefore, husbands and wives must have fewer disagreements and spend more time agreeing on important things for the family.

Long-term planning will require many sacrifices. Both husband and wife will have to make sacrifices if they are planning to achieve certain things in the near future while also working towards their plans. Often, the family may have to do without something, but this sacrifice will allow them to accomplish their long-term plans.

The desire to accomplish long-term plans may cause both husband and wife to seek additional sources of revenue. As a result, either or both of them may have to work extra jobs, or they may have to invest their money to earn additional income.

9.3 Provide suitable alternatives

There are multiple ways to reach the same destination. Husbands must think of different routes to get to the same goal and accomplish the same target. For example, the family may need a vehicle and a house very soon. Instead of purchasing a new vehicle and being unable to afford a house, the family can buy a reconditioned, low-cost car so they can get around while they also pursue acquiring a house. Therefore, they may be able to have the vehicle and the house simultaneously because they have decided how they will spend their money. If they had acquired a new vehicle initially, they might have utilized all of their credit on one item.

Instead of acquiring a vehicle right now, some husbands may decide to utilize public transportation with their wives. Then, within a year, they can use the extra money they have saved to make a significant down payment on a vehicle, or they may be able to buy a vehicle using cash.

9.4 Generate new ideas

In a marriage, the husband must be someone who generates new ideas. There are times when wives may be exhausted with the challenges they face, but husbands ought not to give up too easily.

When children have challenges, they may approach their fathers. Therefore, fathers must be knowledgeable enough to share new ideas with their children and cause them to feel a sense of comfort that their father knows what he is all about.

It can be taxing on the brain to generate new ideas, but husbands may not have to do it every day. Therefore, they should make great use of their time and create new ideas. Then, after they have generated new ideas, husbands must ensure that their ideas materialize.

9.5 Advisor to the wife

A husband must be an excellent advisor to his wife. There are times when she will need sound advice, and he must step in and provide the necessary direction to help his wife accomplish many things. His wife must know that when she approaches him with a concern, he will give her sound advice.

If a wife has to make a financial decision, she can ask her husband for advice. If he does not have immediate answers to share with her, then he must give some thought to the request and think of what can be done as soon as possible. If a husband plans to give his wife feedback, he must honor his word.

10. Investor

A husband must be an investor. He must be willing to invest money wisely, and he must also invest his time and his knowledge into the marriage.

10.1 Investor of money

When people are working for money, they must learn to save and invest some of their earnings. Investments today may produce great rewards for the future.

When considering a monetary investment, persons must know the interest rate. Short-term investments will typically be calculated using simple interest, while long-term investments may be computed using compound interest. Therefore, it is important to understand the difference between these two interest factors.

> If we assume an investment will earn interest only on the original principal, we call this **simple interest.** The process of accumulating interest on an investment over multiple periods is called **compounding**, [and] when interest is earned on both the initial principal and the reinvested interest during prior periods, the result is called **compound interest.** (Titman et al., 2016)

The family's money is a critical resource, and whether it is the husband or the wife who invests such money, they must make sure that there are enough safeguards in place. Persons must be cautious when making their investments in order to avoid Ponzi schemes.

For long-term investment, careful thought must be exercised to know if the investment can be broken in an emergency. With some financial institutions, if assets are broken before the required time, investors will lose their potential interest. In other cases, investors will only receive their interest amount once the investment has matured.

10.2 Invest time with his wife

Husbands must invest in their wives. This includes investments of money, but husbands can also invest time in their wives by sitting down to relax and listen to them. Instead of spending so much time with their friends, they can allocate more time to their wives.

In addition, a husband and wife may go on vacations together, which will be another way to invest time in each other. As part of the vacation, he can take her places she has often longed to go. This simple gesture may cause great interest for a wife, as she once again recognizes that her husband loves her enough to invest in many areas of her life. On the other hand, if a husband acknowledges that his wife is stressed out with family and work-related activities and may need some alone time, he can send her on vacation alone so she can have time to relax and regroup herself.

As investors, husbands must look at key areas to invest in. In addition, it is often expected that the husband's investment in his wife will allow the marriage to have more joy for both persons.

10.3 Invest time with his children

Fathers must invest time in their children, which includes having fun with them. For example, they may spend time watching movies with their children. When fathers attend school meetings with their children, they also show interest in their development. In addition, some fathers will assist their children with schoolwork and assignments.

When children participate in school sports and cultural activities, they will often receive the support of their parents. Fathers may have to take their children to these events, then wait until they are finished and take them home. Children love to know that their fathers are there to support them.

11. Involvement in domestic activities

Domestic activities do not have any gender attached to them. Therefore, both men and women must participate in these tasks at home.

In some families, the wife typically performs most of the domestic activities. However, when the husband participates in these activities, he fulfills his role and adds greater value to their marriage. In addition, as husbands become more engaged in domestic activities, they will be setting a good example for their sons to follow and for their daughters to expect from their future husbands.

Figure 5. Why must men be involved in domestic activities?

With this great example that men will set for their children, it can help to improve many things within the marriage. For instance, in a homes where the wife is mainly responsible for domestic activities, it can often make her tired and frustrated. Traditionally, many wives stayed at home and mainly attended to the needs of their children and husband. However, with changes in economic situations and many women wanting to utilize their skills and knowledge, they are now equally occupied outside the home, just like many men. Therefore, other family members have to take on the responsibility for completing the necessary domestic activities.

Some wives admire their husbands for participating in domestic activities. Many of them will boast to their workmates and families that they have found a gem of a husband who knows how to complete chores without seeking her assistance. However, wives must also understand that they should also participate in domestic activities and not leave everything for their husbands to do. The involvement of both partners in domestic activities will allow them to complete many tasks and give them more time to relax and talk about the important issues of their lives.

Husbands who are good chefs may often talk about their cooking abilities. Some of these husbands will cook, serve the family, and clean up the utensils. On the other hand, some husbands may enjoy cooking but not feel too excited about cleaning the dirty utensils. When a woman has a husband who is good at domestic activities, she must continue to appreciate him and let him know how much she values his involvement. If wives try to suppress their feelings, their husbands may lose focus in doing these important tasks. However, a little encouragement from their wives may make them do more than they initially planned, and soon the marriage will have more excitement.

11.1 Some basic domestic activities for men

In some marriages, the husband may not know to do basic domestic activities at first. However, with a loving wife alongside him, he may begin doing some of the primary domestic activities. Wives must be patient as they teach their husbands to do these tasks.

Figure 6. Some domestic activities for men

Parents can sometimes be blamed for not ensuring that their children learn to do domestic activities while living with them. When children leave their homes and marry but do not know how to do certain basic domestic activities, it strains their marriages.

11.2 Training husbands to be involved in domestic activities

Sometimes, wives will have to take on the responsibility of training their husbands to do domestic activities. This may be a big task, but they will make an effort to do it because when husbands know to do these things, it adds more excellent value to the marriage.

As wives teach their husbands to do domestic activities, they must be patient and remember that they are not teaching their sons. Some husbands may resist learning to do these things, but over time, as their wives engage them to provide support by doing something that is necessary for the family, many of them will become good at these tasks.

As husbands are washing the family clothes, for instance, they must know that clothes may have to be separated based on their color and materials. For example, white clothes will be washed separately from colored clothes. Likewise, clothes may be separated based on their size. For instance, undergarments may be washed separately from pants, dresses, bedsheets, or other items. Therefore, husbands must not be afraid to wash clothing of all types and sizes, even the smallest undergarments that their wives wear. A husband who knows to take care of his wife's clothing may be treated as the king in the home, since his wife knows that she cannot find any other man as good as her husband. Therefore, husbands, do good things for your family, especially your wife, and you may have long and happy days with her.

11.3 Congratulating husbands for their involvement in domestic activities

Many husbands look forward to any compliment they can get, especially from their wives, whenever they do any domestic activities. These compliments may inspire them to do more domestic activities, which will bring great joy to the hearts of their wives.

When a wife compliments her husband for anything good he has done, it must not be followed by a complaint about something he has not done. A wife's compliment to a husband must come from her heart and be allowed to resonate with him. He must be motivated to do more good things regularly.

In the same way that a wife expects gifts and reasonable treatment from her husband, she must also do the same things for him. She must let him know that he is a great husband to her and that she appreciates what he is doing.

11.4 Shopping lists

As a provider to the family, some husbands will give their financial contributions to their wives. In addition, they may ask their wives to manage the things that have to be purchased in the home. However, some men were well trained by their parents, so they know how to prepare a shopping list. Therefore, they know how to manage the family money very well by looking for bargains.

If a husband does not know how to prepare a shopping list, his wife can prepare a list and give it to him to purchase groceries, vegetables, and meats. Some wives will also go to the extent of telling their husbands where they can go to get the groceries.

In some families, on weekends or whenever both partners have time, they will go to the markets and supermarkets together. When this happens, husbands who did not know how to purchase certain items will learn where those items are located and how much each one costs.

Some husbands are very good at shopping for the family. They often negotiate the prices for certain items to get discounts, and they are willing to shop at different places to save the family a few dollars. Some men may choose to purchase in bulk to benefit from lower unit prices for each item.

11.5 Identifying where items are stored in the house

Husbands must be aware of where items are stored in the house so that when they are doing domestic activities, they know where to get those things and where to put them back. For example, if men are going to wash clothes, they must know where the clothespins are, and after the clothes are collected from the lines, the clothespins have to be returned to the correct location.

When husbands have to cook, they must know where the necessary household items are, without calling their wives when they need anything. After they finish preparing a meal, they may gather the family around the table and serve them, remembering to help the family with a smile.

While domestic activities may not be an everyday thing for most men, they must do it with joy. They must know that any contribution they make for their family is also doing something good for themselves.

12. Fathering the children

Caring for children is not an easy job. It requires the help and support of many persons, but mainly the father and mother. Other family members may support them at times, but parents must not depend on relatives to be fully responsible for their children.

When both parents are involved in the care and development of their children, the children will likely learn to respect both parents. In addition, it eases the challenges that one parent would have to go through to provide for and nurture the children alone.

Looking after the children is never a matter of gender. However, children sometimes cling to their mothers if their fathers do not spend enough time with them. It is understood that the nature of some fathers' work may cause them to be busy and away from home frequently, but whenever they are available, they need to spend time with their children.

Figure 7. Why fathers must spend time with their children

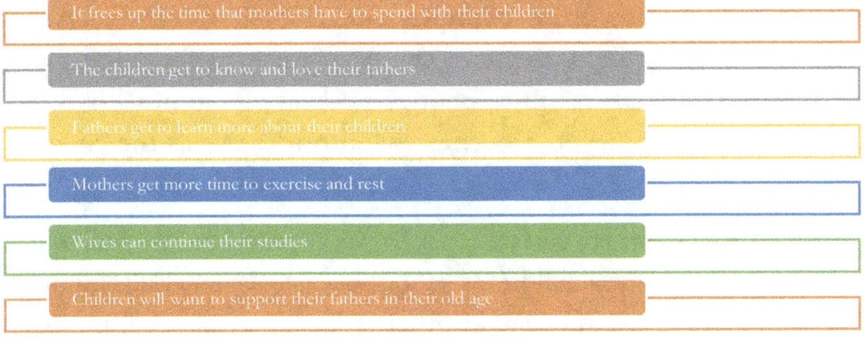

12.1 It frees up the time that mothers have to spend with their children

One of the big things that some mothers want is for their husbands to spend more time with the children. Domestic activities and attending to children can take up most of the parents' time. However, when the husband is involved, many of the activities that one parent would be doing can now be shared between the two of them. Many wives look forward to the day when their husbands will be providing guidance and support to their children.

12.2 The children get to know and love their fathers

When fathers spend more time with their children, the children get to know more about them. As a result, many children become attached to their fathers and love them.

Fathers who are there for their children must be complimented. These fathers will teach their children to cook for the family and watch movies with them. When they are at home, their wives know that they can rest because the children will be so connected with their father that they almost forget their mother is at home.

12.3 Fathers get to learn more about their children

As fathers spend more time with their children, they learn more about them and will see how their children are developing over the years. As the children grow in height and weight, fathers will notice those developments and spend more money purchasing clothes for them. The funds to be spent on groceries will also increase as the children grow.

When children's school performance has increased, fathers will know this as they check their children's school books. When children know that their parents are interested in their education, they will improve their educational performance.

12.4 Mothers get more time to exercise and rest

Mothers who want to exercise will have more time to do so when their husbands attend to the children. While their husbands are with the children, wives may also have more time to rest or to visit the salon and have themselves adequately cared for.

12.5 Wives can continue their studies

Wives who are studying or who want to study may be better able to increase their education if their husbands spend more time with the children. It can often be difficult to give much attention to children and focus on one's studies at the same time. Many wives have not pursued their dreams to study after getting married because too much focus had to be placed on attending to the needs of the children. However, when husbands are there for the children, their wives can continue studying.

12.6 Children will want to support their fathers in their old age

Parents must remember that they will not remain young all the days of their lives. Therefore, if they invest time with their children, their children will want to support them when they get older. Thus, fathers must capitalize on this opportunity to spend quality time with their children so that in their more senior years, their children will be alongside them and give them much support.

13. Lover of his wife

If a husband does not love his wife and she does not love him, then the marriage is just a public spectacle. Love must be complementary for both persons: the husband must show an interest in his wife and reciprocate her interest or acceptance of him. Too often, when one partner is making all the effort to reach out to the other one, it strains the marriage, and very soon, they may be arguing with each other.

13.1 Single focus on his wife

When a husband is married but is still thinking of another woman, he will not fully commit to the marriage. Also, the wife has to have a single focus on her husband, because if she does not, it can be frustrating and may drive him to give more attention to someone outside of the marriage.

When husbands focus on their wives, they will try to avoid things that will distract them from their marriage, since they cannot break the trust that their wives have in them.

Some men do types of work that involve much interaction with other women. Nevertheless, they must be responsible and committed to their wives, ignoring all opportunities available to them that could jeopardize their marriage. They must know that they will hurt their wives and themselves if they do anything to violate their marriage.

Either the husband or the wife may become caught up in the generous offer of someone outside of the marriage. For example, those who are involved in sports may have a close physical connection with persons of the opposite gender as they practice or participate in the sport. However, they must consider that if they do anything to harm their marriage, their partner may do a similar thing, and they will not like such actions.

13.2 Being romantic with his wife

Husbands are expected to be romantic with their wives. They must use all of their energy and time to have an effect on their partners. Being romantic does not always mean that the result will be sex. However, many wives love for their husbands to express their emotions. Some husbands will say just the right words to their wives to make them feel joyful and feel a sense of belonging to the marriage.

On many occasions, verbal communication is important for husbands and wives to be romantic. Husbands are expected to say soothing words to their wives, since that may be the icebreaker for their romantic relationship. In Song of Solomon chapter 6, King Solomon provides some choice words to help men communicate with their wives.

Song of Solomon 4:10-15

[10] How fair is thy love, my sister, my spouse! how much better is thy love than wine! and the smell of thine ointments than all spices! [11] Thy lips, O my spouse, drop as the honeycomb: honey and milk are under thy tongue; and the smell of thy garments is like the smell of Lebanon. [12] A garden inclosed is my sister, my spouse; a spring shut up, a fountain sealed. [13] Thy plants are an orchard of pomegranates, with pleasant fruits; camphire, with spikenard, [14] Spikenard and saffron; calamus and cinnamon, with all trees of frankincense; myrrh and aloes, with all the chief spices: [15] A fountain of gardens, a well of living waters, and streams from Lebanon.

Husbands must behave with their wives as though they were still on their honeymoon. Naturally, therefore, there will be much excitement in the marriage as each partner shows affection.

Husbands must be willing to go anywhere with their wives. As they go places, they can hold hands or hug each other. They cannot be afraid to demonstrate their appreciation and affection for each other.

However, they must not hold hands while driving, since this is a traffic violation.

13.3 Dinner dates

When many couples were going through courtship, they had dinner dates, but once they are married, they forget to make their marriage exciting. To rediscover that excitement, husbands can organize dinner dates with their wives, where they plan to go and have dinner at a place where they are comfortable. If they have young children, they will have to arrange for someone to watch them while they are on their dinner date. Too often, husbands and wives focus too much on the children and forget each other. Husbands and wives sometimes need to move their focus away from their children and have dinner dates together away from home, since there are a variety of benefits in dining out.

Figure 8. Advantages for couples dining away from home

13.4 Dancing together

Husbands and wives do not need to be professional dancers to dance together. If they practice dancing together at home, they may become better when dancing together in public. As they dance at home, they can choose whatever songs they are comfortable with. As they dance, they can even sing along with the songs. When couples dance at home, they can relax or go to bed if they are tired.

13.5 Avoiding intruders

It is crucial for a husband to say no to any intruders into the marriage. There are so many easy ways for husbands or wives to become involved in extramarital affairs, so they must avoid falling into such a trap. First, therefore, they must look out for the devices of the intruders and put up their stop signs.

Suppose a husband senses that a conversation may go in a particular direction that will invade his marriage. In that case, he must be strong-willed enough to discontinue the conversation or change the topic. Sometimes, the conversation may sound sweet to his ears, but continuing the discussion can be one of the most dangerous decisions he will ever make.

13.6 Buying romantic clothes for her

Some husbands are ashamed to be seen in public purchasing certain clothes for their wives, thinking that others will look down on them. However, every husband must do whatever it takes to make his wife know that he loves her beyond the shadow of a doubt. She must hear him talking about his love towards her, and she must also see him demonstrating that in so many places.

When wives feel comfortable with the clothes that their husbands have purchased for them, they walk with a sense of pride and comfort that they are wearing clothes that their husbands have fully approved. In some marriages, the husband is not always comfortable with all of the wife's clothes. But when he purchases the clothes for her, she knows that he cannot question her decision of what to wear.

A husband must also know his wife's size in order to purchase clothes for her. If not, he may buy an exotic piece of clothing for much money, only to find that it does not fit her properly. When husbands spend cash to purchase clothes for their wives, many wives appreciate what their husbands have done for them.

13.7 Let her know regularly that you love her

The marriage between a husband and wife is not a one-day event. Husbands must constantly let their wives know that they love them. If wives are working, they must leave their homes each day knowing that their husbands love them.

When a husband leaves home and goes to another place where his wife is not with him, then if he can call her after he reaches his destination, he must do so. If he is required to spend multiple days at that location, he can call his wife most days, if not every day, and inquire about how she and the children are doing. He must let her know that he loves her during each conversation.

14. Romance and sex

In every relationship between a husband and wife, romance and sex are important concerns. Oftentimes, at the initial stage of the relationship, the couple discusses romance and sex more than planning to build a house.

14.1 Deprivation of romance and sex

When one partner chooses to deprive the other of sex, it often creates unease in the relationship. This unease may lead to separation or divorce. However, believers are expected to set good examples for others to see and follow.

The Apostle Paul provides information to guide believers about their romantic and sexual lives. While there are times when it will be necessary for a married couple to abstain from sex, it cannot become a permanent thing, since that can lead to the destruction of the marriage.

1 Corinthians 7:1-7

[1] Now concerning the things whereof ye wrote unto me: It is good for a man not to touch a woman. [2] Nevertheless, to avoid fornication, let every man have his own wife, and let every woman have her own husband. [3] Let the husband render unto the wife due benevolence: and likewise also the wife unto the husband. [4] The wife hath not power of her own body, but the husband: and likewise also the husband hath not power of his own body, but the wife. [5] Defraud ye not one the other, except it be with consent for a time, that ye may give yourselves to fasting and prayer; and come together again, that Satan tempt you not for your incontinency. [6] But I speak this by permission, and not of commandment. [7] For I would that all men were even

as I myself. But every man hath his proper gift of God, one after this manner, and another after that.

14.2 Make the relationship romantic

Believers must make their relationship romantic. As much as believers love the Lord, husbands and wives must set aside enough time for each other and make their lovemaking a priority for them. When there is much love in the relationship, partners do not have as much time to think about problems. On the other hand, if couples allow their problems to consume them, then the sexual relationship will be affected.

Hebrews 13:4

[4] Marriage is honourable in all, and the bed undefiled: but whoremongers and adulterers God will judge.

The entire book of the Song of Solomon is important for married couples to read. It will awaken their sensual relationship and make their marriage happy. It may also prevent intruders from entering their relationship and thereby reduce the number of divorces among Christian couples.

15. Studying his wife

Studying one's wife can be a very challenging thing for many husbands to do. For a husband, it may be easier to study for an examination and pass it than to study his wife.

15.1 There is always more to learn

Husbands must be aware that they will never know everything about their wives. While a man may have been married to his wife for many years, women will periodically change the way they think about certain issues. They may like one type of food today, but then dislike the same food a few days from now. If they design the house in one way now, they might choose to rearrange it before the year ends. For example, the bed and closet will be positioned in one direction, and before the year is completed, the wife will ask her husband for assistance in rearranging the furniture.

When women are younger, they may enjoy wearing high-heeled shoes. However, as they have children or they age, they may prefer to wear shoes with a lower heel. Similarly, not all men may be big on fashion and designer clothes, but some women will change quickly with new fashion trends.

A husband will never know everything about his wife, but he needs to know some things about her. He has to be observant and read her non-verbal communication. If he attempts to ask too many questions of her, he needs to know that he may not always get all the answers he needs.

15.2 Know her family history

When a man marries a woman, he must know that he also becomes connected to her family. She may behave similarly to her other family members. For example, if her parents and siblings like to laugh and have conversations with people, she may bring the same culture to the marriage. If members of her family often want to isolate themselves from people and public events, she may display similar characteristics in her marriage.

When wives come from wealthy parents, they may not be afraid to spend large sums of money to acquire things they like. Therefore, the husband of such a wife is expected to have much money to meet her needs, or he may have to train her to adjust her spending. Wives who come from families with strong academic backgrounds may often want to pursue their studies and never be satisfied with having only the basic certificates.

There are some wives whose background involved many outdoor activities. Therefore, they will expect to have similar treatment when they enter marriage. When it comes to domestic activities, not every wife will enjoy washing, pressing, or folding clothes. Therefore, the couple will have to decide who will do certain chores. During courtship, a man should seek to know some of these things about his future wife.

15.3 Know what makes her sad

Certain things will make many women sad. For example, gender-based violence will make women miserable, even if it has not happened to them personally. However, there are some unique things for each woman that will make her sad. Therefore, each husband must know what can cause his wife to be sad and try to avoid those things.

15.4 Know what makes her happy

There are also certain things that will make many wives happy. A husband has to learn about those things and do something to make his wife happy whenever the need arises. For example, wives who like to spend most of their time at home may watch family movies, and they will often want their husbands to watch with them. When their husbands are alongside them, they may feel secure or have more time to talk about things that are affecting them.

15.5 Learn about her friends

Not all wives will have many friends, but they will certainly have at least one. Therefore, a husband needs to know his wife's friends and allow her to have some free space with them, as long as her friends are not bad influences on the marriage. In addition, some of her friends may be from her childhood days, so they will have many things to talk about.

15.6 Learn about the movies she likes

While many men will like to watch sports, political news, and other things that interest them, they also need to know what movies their wives like to watch, and they must make themselves available to watch them together. Some wives want to be in their husband's arms while they watch movies, so he is expected to be at home when he does not have to work. Some wives will watch movies that will help them be better equipped to deal with their marriage. They do not watch movies just for fun but also to learn what they can do to improve their marriage. Similarly, some wives will watch cooking shows in order to learn to prepare better meals.

16. Respecting his wife

Each partner in a marriage must respect the other one if they want their marriage to be joyful and long-lasting. There may be many things that will cause differences between them, but they must maintain their respect for each other.

16.1 There will be disagreements

In every marriage, there will be disagreements. No marriage will be free from differences. Sometimes, through differences, the truth may be revealed. Conflict may allow one person to see the emotional response of their partner, whether they choose to cry or be silent.

However, no one must provoke their partner to have regular disagreements. Provocation can lead to significant disputes that may never be resolved. In addition, too much stimulation may result in one person harming both themself and their partner.

Colossians 3:19

[19] Husbands, love your wives, and be not bitter against them.

Sometimes, these disagreements will stem from minor issues or misunderstandings. First, however, each partner must find the root cause of their conflicts and find ways to keep those areas of disagreement from repeating. For example, parents may have disagreements about their children's behaviors, where one partner allows the children to do most of the things they want to do, while the other disagrees with the children's actions.

16.2 Forgiveness is important for both persons

To foster respect in the marriage, both persons must forgive each other and put aside their differences. Christian families know that forgiveness is essential for them, so they ought to follow their religious teachings.

Ephesians 4:32

[32] And be ye kind one to another, tenderhearted, forgiving one another, even as God for Christ's sake hath forgiven you.

The longer both partners hold disagreements in their hearts, the more they will cause themselves to lose hope in themselves and the marriage. When there are disagreements, one partner may choose to limit their conversations with the other, and limited discussion can create room for speculation. Critical decisions may have to be delayed because both partners have not agreed to discuss certain matters. The longer partners take to forgive each other, the more time they allow to pass without reconciliation, and many opportunities may go wasted because they have chosen not to talk frequently due to a disagreement.

Therefore, at least one partner must be mature enough to seek to forgive the other and reconcile their differences. It will take much courage, but it will be important to keep the marriage alive.

16.3 Seek counseling

If the disagreements persist, both persons should seek counseling. This will show their willingness to have others intervene to help them to resolve their disagreements. No partner must believe that being too weak to deal with family problems is what has led them to seek counseling. Rather, they should recognize that they are seeking counseling because they want a mutual person to help them identify and resolve their disagreements.

16.4 Respect her within the home

Both partners must respect each other at home. They must live lovingly with each other within the house so that when they are outside of the home, they are themselves and not trying to act to impress the public. Of course, they will have disagreements, but their quick response to agree and live in peace must be something they practice daily.

Husbands, look for opportunities to keep building your marriage. Give your wife the respect she deserves. Do not measure her against the children, and do not give more consideration to the children than to your wife. You may not like everything she does and says, but you must still respect her.

When children see their fathers respecting their mothers, they may want to follow a similar pattern when they have their own families. Therefore, each family must try to raise children who will be good role models and practice those good qualities that their parents demonstrated within the home.

Husbands must know their wives' needs and work to meet them. They must understand what makes their wives uncomfortable and avoid those things or areas of discussion. Husbands must listen to their wives and keep giving them the support they deserve whenever they want to do good things. The husband must not let his wife feel like she is a stranger to the home. She must not feel as though she is the second woman in the marriage; at all times, she must know and sense that she is his one and only partner.

16.5 Respect her outside of the home

Husbands must love their wives both at home and outside the home, demonstrating respect to them whenever they are in public together. Husbands may not always agree with the decisions their wives will make in public places, but they must be tactful in responding to anything they disagree with. A husband's body language can sometimes communicate if he agrees or disagrees with his wife's actions in public.

Both partners must not shout or walk away when they disagree with one another, especially in public places. When both partners learn to live well with each other at home, it may be a natural thing for them to do when they are in public as well. If a husband disagrees with something his wife has done in public, he must look for appropriate times and places to suggest the approach she should have taken in that situation.

17. Helping her to stay healthy and in shape

Both partners must commit to keeping each other healthy in the marriage. Sometimes, wives may have to help their husbands to be in shape. Nevertheless, husbands must also be there for their wives and ensure that they eat healthy food and find ways to exercise.

Figure 9. Why husbands must help their wives to stay healthy and in shape

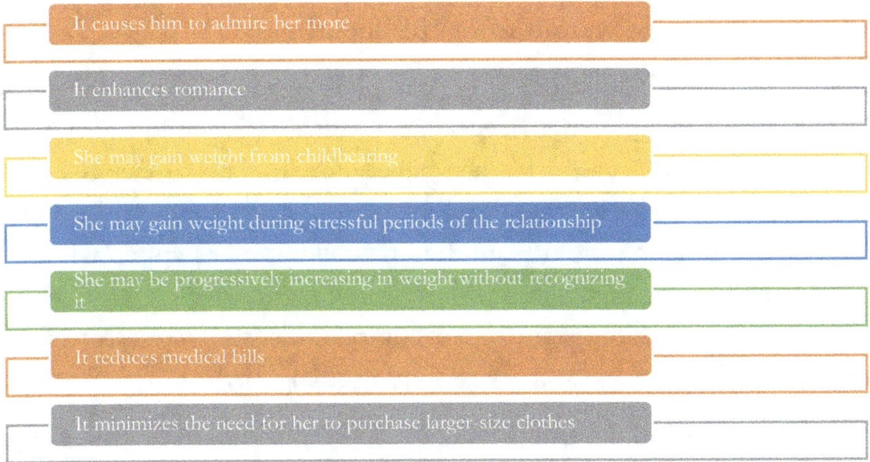

17.1 It causes him to admire her more

Men love to admire women; there is no doubt about that. However, husbands ought to respect their wives. They must have a single focus, placing all of their attention on their wives.

In addition to saying beautiful words to her, a husband must look at his wife's physical structure and shape and let her know how beautifully made she is. A husband telling his wife about her gorgeous body must not be a one-off event or only done on special occasions. Rather, it must become his new song after he marries her, as he has a responsibility to help her maintain that enchanting look.

17.2 It enhances romance

Because each marriage involves an emotional and physical response, the wife's looks must appeal to her husband. As a result, many wives have taken great care to ensure that they still maintain decent shapes for their husbands' benefit and contribute to the romance of their marriages.

What the eyes can see in a marriage often triggers the mind. So, husbands, help your wife be the woman you will constantly look at. It may be hard work to help her stay in shape, but it is a worthwhile investment and sacrifice for the benefit of the marriage.

17.3 She may gain weight from childbearing

Sometimes, a wife automatically gains much weight after giving birth to her first child. Some marriages may produce many children within a short period, and wives may not have enough time to exercise and reduce any increase in size from the previous delivery. While some wives may not gain weight from the first child, it may happen with the other children. Unfortunately, wives gain weight after giving birth in areas with a sensual appeal to their companions, so every effort must be made to lose unnecessary weight after giving birth.

17.4 She may gain weight during stressful periods of the marriage

Wives who are going through stressful marriages may choose to eat more. They may also choose not to exercise as much as they used to because they do not feel mentally prepared for it. If they do not pay attention, they may increase in weight within a short time because they have been eating much more during this stressful period. Therefore, husbands, see what you can do to minimize stress, and also encourage your wife to watch her weight and help her to exercise. She may be too mentally stressed to fight off the weight increase by herself, so you may need to go with her for routine exercise or purchase exercise equipment to help her stay in shape.

17.5 She may be progressively increasing in weight without recognizing it

Over the years, most wives will recognize that they are no longer at the weight they had when they first got married. Whether they have children or not, they may constantly increase their weight over time. It may be because their husbands are great chefs and often cook their favorite food and give them large portions. It may also be that both partners have received increases in their compensation, so they also increase their grocery spending and are consuming larger meals.

17.6 It reduces medical bills

When husbands help their wives to be healthy, they are working towards keeping their family medical bills low. With a significant increase in weight, however, will come some health issues. Therefore, every attempt that husbands can make to keep their wives and themselves healthy and in shape may result in having more money to spend on other important areas in the marriage.

17.7 It minimizes the need for her to purchase larger-size clothes

Women like to look good in the clothes they wear. Many times, they will buy clothes that cause persons to admire them. However, when wives constantly increase their weight, they will have to get new clothing in larger sizes. This can be a costly exercise, since they may have to replace most of the clothes in their closets.

17.8 Healthy diet

Husbands, do whatever you can to ensure that you contribute to your wife's healthy eating. She may like to eat many meals that are tasty but not necessarily nutritious, so you must be there to remind her to stay healthy. When husbands visit the markets and supermarkets to purchase groceries, they must buy healthy products for the family.

Husbands must know what contributes to a balanced diet and have most of those items within the home.

Table 5. There are five main groups of nutrients

Main groups of nutrients	Explanation	Sources of the nutrients
Protein	The primary function of protein is to provide body-building or growth materials, so every cell in the body contains proteins.	Meat, fish, cheese, eggs, wheat, rice, oats, beans
Fat (and oil)	Provides a convenient and concentrated source of energy, supplying more energy than the same weight of carbohydrate or protein.	Meat, butter, margarine, fish, nuts, fruits
Carbohydrate	Carbohydrates are the most important source of energy for the body. Almost all the cells of the body use glucose to distribute energy. Carbohydrate acts as a "protein sparer" so that protein can be used for its primary functions rather than as a source of energy.	Sugar, honey, molasses, jam, jelly, yam, sweet potato, breadfruit, rice, barley, corn
Vitamins	Vitamins are a group of chemical substances, most of which were identified during the 20th century as vital to the body. The body requires only	Milk, cheese, eggs, carrot, spinach, watercress, cabbage,

	small amounts of each vitamin. Vitamins can be classified according to the substances in which they dissolve.	tomato, pumpkin, Callao, cod liver oil
Minerals	Bodybuilding. Control of bodily processes. Essential parts of body fluid. Some mineral elements are required in relatively large amounts.	Milk, cheese, broccoli, bok choy, legumes, bread

(Extract from Tull & Coward, 2009)

Every now and again, the family may want to consume a meal that deviates from a balanced diet, but this practice must not become the norm. Husbands must purchase foods that contain the nutrients listed in the table above, and when they are preparing meals, most meals must contain these important nutrients.

17.9 Exercising

Both husbands and wives must exercise. Based on their schedule, they can make exercising a routine activity for them. When husbands help their wives to exercise, it may act as a motivator for them. They may want to be competitive with their husbands and exercise as often as possible.

As a married couple goes on walks together, whether in the parks or in their communities, they will have time to discuss important matters, such as their challenges at work. There are many benefits when couples exercise together. For example, if they set targets of reducing their weight by a certain amount or percentage, they may hold each other accountable for reaching that target very soon.

Persons who are exercising need the support and motivation of others. Husbands may encourage their wives to continue exercising, as the love of their lives is right beside them. They may even feel secure exercising with their husbands and not feel ashamed about performing certain routines. For example, if a couple can dance, they can play songs that they like, and they will be exercising as they move while listening to those songs. If the types of exercises they do require much physical contact with another person, the wife will be comfortable having her husband there just with her.

18. Celebrator of his wife

Husbands, if you want to enjoy your marriage, one thing you are expected to do is to make your wife feel special. There are so many ways to make wives feel unique, and each husband must assess how he can do this for his wife. The formula for making one husband's wife feel special may not be the one that will work for another couple. Each wife will react in her own way when her husband makes her feel special.

Every partner must understand that they are working towards a happy marriage. Of course, this happiness will not happen in just one moment; rather, it may take a buildup of many things to make a wife happy.

Wives, when your husband makes you feel special, acknowledge his effort and contributions. Let him know that you appreciate what he has done to make you feel special. If you hide your feelings, he may not want to try doing anything significant because he thinks you do not appreciate what he has done.

18.1 Remember her birthday

Wives sometimes complain that their husbands do not remember their birthdays. This can be a troubling experience for them, since celebrating birthdays is essential.

Figure 10. Ways for a husband to remember his wife's birthday

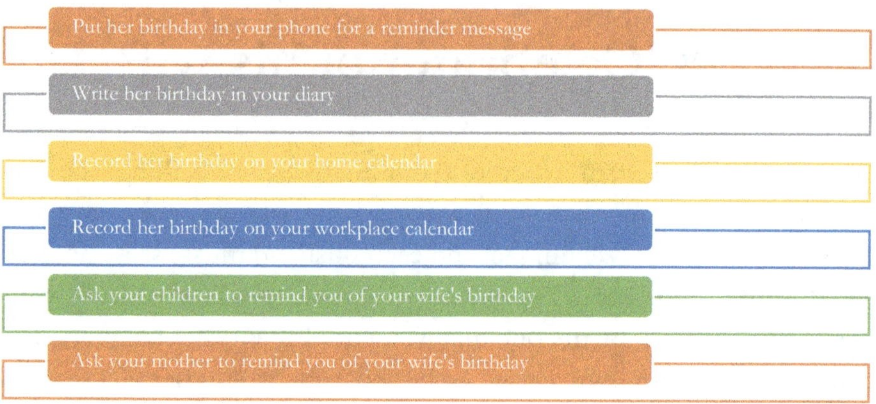

Not all husbands are good at remembering their wives' birthdays. Wives ought to forgive their husbands if they forget that important date, but husbands must still make a special effort to remember it. If a husband forgets on a few occasions, he may be forgiven, but he cannot forget all the time, since this would reflect a lack of interest in remembering his wife's birthday.

If a husband knows that he may not remember his wife's birthday off the top of his head, he will need to record that important date somewhere so that he can remember when it is approaching. For example, he can write it down on his calendar or other places he frequently visits. These reminders may allow him to purchase whatever gift he wants to give to his wife or remember to take her someplace she wants to go to celebrate this great day.

A husband may be able to trust his mother and siblings to remind him of his wife's birthday, or perhaps he can ask his children to remind him. While this approach may not be ideal, the most important thing is that husbands do not want to forget their wives' birthdays. The nature of some husbands' work may keep them far away from home on a regular basis, so they may not be able to commit their wives' birthdays to memory.

18.2 Celebrate her birthday

Besides just knowing when his wife's birthday is, a husband must celebrate it. This may start with a simple acknowledgment in the morning, along with a birthday card, and then later in the day, it may include lunch and dinner. It can also involve taking her on vacation or purchasing jewelry and other assets that make her feel special. She must know that her husband is not ashamed to celebrate with her, and that he is not afraid to spend money to make her feel special on that day.

18.3 Celebrate wedding anniversaries

In addition to birthdays, husbands must also celebrate their wedding anniversaries. The first wedding anniversary may be a great accomplishment for both partners. After that, they may be excited to celebrate the fifth wedding anniversary, and probably every five years after that. However they choose to celebrate their wedding anniversary, it must be something that they both enjoy and love.

Some wedding anniversaries can be celebrated right at home, and others may be celebrated somewhere else. However, when couples have children and have invested their money to acquire vehicles and houses, they may want to consider the cost of these celebrations, since they have significant expenses to take care of.

18.4 Celebrate her promotions

If a woman is promoted, her husband should celebrate that moment with her. It may be her dedication and knowledge that gave her the opportunity to be promoted. For a woman to be promoted within her organization, she may have to perform exceptionally well and be dedicated to her job, perhaps leaving home early most mornings to go to work.

These other celebrations often make wives feel valued in the marriage. Wives like to know that their husbands are there with them during both difficult times and good times.

18.5 Celebrate her examination successes

Just like men, women will spend time studying. After completing their examinations, they often look forward to celebrating these accomplishments. Therefore, a husbands can join in with his wife to celebrate her success in her examinations. This may cause her to want to increase her academics further, which will make her more marketable.

The educational accomplishments of some wives will be beneficial for the family, especially when the children have schoolwork to complete. In addition, if the family has a business, then the wife can use the knowledge she gains to support that business.

18.6 Celebrate her as the wife of your children

If wives do not conceive and give birth, husbands will not be fathers, and not every wife will be able to conceive. Therefore, husbands must make their wives feel special for the children they give birth to.

Women's challenges in carrying each child in the womb are not easy. The experience in the labor room is another unforgettable time for many wives, yet they go through the process for the benefit of the entire family.

18.7 Celebrate her on national and international women's days

There are several international days to celebrate women, including Mother's Day. Whatever the celebration is, if it has anything to do with women, include your wife and make her feel special.

Your wife must know that you are always there to celebrate her. She must have more seasons of joy and fewer seasons of stress, so be her biggest supporter in her life.

Section 3: Celebrating husbands

Husbands are humans and deserve to be celebrated, especially if they are fulfilling their godly responsibilities. Therefore, it is essential to celebrate every husband, particularly since children and wives cannot achieve the roles that husbands perform.

Wives must encourage their children to make their fathers feel special regularly. No wife must be ashamed to celebrate her husband, since she loves him and does not leave room for other women to gain his interest. The works that many Christian husbands do must be celebrated, since they are very involved in the work of the Lord while also providing for their families.

Husbands' birthdays may be an excellent time to celebrate them. On a couple's wedding anniversary, the husband must be celebrated alongside his wife.

19. Compliment and congratulate husbands

Now that you know the primary roles of husbands, you are better informed to appreciate them. If husbands are performing their roles, then they must be complimented. It is often seen that persons celebrate women whenever they do certain things. However, men must also be celebrated, which will give them the strength to continue being the great husbands they are.

No one must look to any husband as perfect, of course, since all humans have shortcomings. Nevertheless, when husbands perform their roles without looking for praise, their wives and children must celebrate them. On their birthdays, they must be celebrated by those who know them best. Furthermore, every day should be seen as a day to celebrate husbands who know and perform their roles.

19.1 Set an example for sons to follow

Many sons pay attention how their fathers are being treated. If their fathers are treated as significant people, they will follow a similar example when they are older, wanting to be a husband like their father. When wives celebrate their husbands, sons often take note of those responses.

19.2 Teach other women to honor their husbands

Women who are not married may look for wives to set good examples for them. Therefore, when they see wives treating their husbands with love and respect, they have some good examples to follow. As role models, wives can encourage other women to get married and make their husbands feel celebrated.

19.3 Make him feel like a king every day

A husband must know and feel every day that he is a king. He must not search for reasons to wonder if his wife and his children love him. He must constantly hear good things from his wife. She must want him to return home every day, and when he is at home, he must be treated as the best and only man in her life. She must make him have no interest in any other women he sees, because she has demonstrated that no other woman can match her characteristics. The way she celebrates her husband must cause him to be thankful for marrying her.

No husband is perfect, but good treatment may make some husbands improve their performance and behavior. The few kind words said to a husband as he faithfully executes his role may be just what he was longing to hear. When wives make their husbands feel like kings, those kings will soon make their wives feel like queens. Therefore, both persons in a marriage must start celebrating each other today and not procrastinate.

Reference list

Cole, G. A. (1993). *Management theory and practice* (4th ed.). DP Publications.

Givens, P., Hunte, P., Quan-Kep, Y., & Morris, M. (2010). *Human and social biology for CSEC*. Nelson Thornes.

Hughes, R., Ginnett, R. & Curphy, G. (2015). *Leadership: Enhancing the lessons of experience* (8th ed.). McGraw-Hill Education.

Smith, S. (1988). *Sandra Smith's review for NCLEX-RN*. National Nursing Review, Inc.

Titman, S., Martin, T., Keown, A. J., & Martin, J. D. (2016). *Financial management: Principles and applications* (7th ed.). Pearson Australia.

Tull, A., & Coward, A. (2009). *Caribbean food and nutrition for CSEC*. Oxford University Press.

About the author

Rev. Geary Reid was asked to make a virtual presentation on 26 November 2021, at midnight, to an international audience on the subject of "The Husband's Role." This virtual presentation had attendees from several continents and was coordinated and hosted by Joanne Harte, Ralph Harte, Sandra Salome Daniels-Harte, and Pastor Nadine Grigsby. The focus of this presentation was to provide the listeners with a better understanding of the husband's role in a marriage. To prepare for the presentation, Reid searched through his previous books for information about the husband's role, and he recognized that he had never addressed this subject before. He then decided to explore other places for literature to make this a more impactful discussion. Even as he searched for pertinent things to share in the virtual presentation, he recognized that there was limited information on this subject matter.

Reid used scripture and academic information as his guides for this important teaching session. He also decided to use his own experience as a husband, which spans more than two decades. Remembering roles he saw his father demonstrate, he also incorporated those into the discussion. As a religious leader and former president of the Men's Fellowship, Rev. Geary Reid eventually knew that he had enough practical and biblical information to share with the international audience. Therefore, immediately after giving his virtual presentation, he decided to prepare this literature to help readers understand the roles of Christian husbands.

In this literature, Reid provides academic and religious information combined with practical experiences as a husband. He constantly interacts with many husbands and wives, and he understands the difficulty of understanding what husbands are expected to do. The roles of Christian husbands must also be understood through the eyes of their wives.

Reid knows that he is not a perfect husband, but he often strives to better understand the important roles he must play as a believer within the home as he works to meet the family's needs. He has watched movies that provide additional information to help him perform better as a husband. In discussing these issues with other husbands and men older than him, he has been able to glean from their wisdom.

The roles of Christian husbands are many, and Rev. Geary Reid is still looking to be more effective in those areas in which he has shortcomings. However, he often encourages husbands to do the right things, since their mistakes can affect entire generations.

Christian husbands who were not familiar with their roles now have an opportunity to become aware of these roles and be good husbands to the wives they have chosen. Christian wives also need to learn their husbands' roles so that they do not have unrealistic expectations of them. Altogether, Reid wants to see more marriages grow as husbands and wives work together so that their children have good mentors to follow.